Michel Marie
THE FRENCH
NEW WAVE
An Artistic School
Translated by Richard Neupert

Blackwell
Publishing

350 Main Street, Malden, MA 02148-5018, USA
108 Cowley Road, Oxford OX4 1JF, UK
550 Swanston Street, Carlton, Victoria 3053, Australia
Kurfürstendamm 57, 10707 Berlin, Germany

First published 1997 as *La Nouvelle Vague: Une école artistique* by Editions NATHAN,
Paris

This translation first published 2003 by Blackwell Publishers Ltd, a Blackwell
Publishing company

Library of Congress Cataloging-in-Publication Data

Marie, Michel, 1945–
[Nouvelle vague. English]
The French new wave : an artistic school / Michel Marie ; translated
by Richard Neupert.
    p. cm.
Includes bibliographical references and index. ISBN 0-631-22657-5 (hardcover : alk.
paper)—ISBN 0-631-22658-3 (pbk. : alk. paper)
1. Motion pictures—France—History. 2. New wave films—France—History.
I. Neupert, Richard John. II. Title.
PN1993.5.F7 M2713 2002
791.43'0944—dc21
        2002004420

A catalogue record for this title is available from the British Library.

Set in Fournier
by SNP Best-set Typesetter Ltd., Hong Kong
Printed and bound in the United Kingdom
by T.J. International, Padstow, Cornwall

For further information on
Blackwell Publishers, visit our website:
www.blackwellpublishers.co.uk

Contents

Translator's Note

WHEN CITING FILM TITLES for this introductory-level history of the French New Wave, in first references I have included in most cases both the original French title and then the predominant English-language title. When the distributed print generally retains the French title, as is the case with *Hiroshima mon amour*, I have left it in French, though I do provide a translation in parentheses, to aid non-French speakers. However, part of the importance of Michel Marie's book is that it cites a great many movies from the 1950s which, while popular in France, may never have received widespread distribution, and therefore do not have any official English-language title; in those cases I provide a literal translation of the title. It is also worth noting that the title given to a movie in the UK is sometimes very different from its equivalent in the United States. I generally retain the title that has become most common in other histories, though some films have been so dramatically changed from the French that I retain all release titles to aid in their recognition, as in the case of *La Traversée de Paris*, which was given the unfortunate titles of *Four Bags Full* for its US release, but *Pigs across Paris* in the UK! Marie's original text did not include notes; I have added them for clarification of sources where necessary.

Richard Neupert

Introduction

THE FRENCH NOUVELLE VAGUE AGAIN!

The Nouvelle Vague, or New Wave, is certainly one of the most famous cinematic movements in film history. Scholars continually refer to it with either nostalgia or some suspicion. As early as 1959, the uncle in *Zazie dans le métro* (*Zazie in the Metro*, Malle) looked about in the middle of a traffic jam in Paris and screamed out ironically, "This is the New Wave!" But what, finally, *is* the New Wave?

Beyond the mythical "circle of friends," the famed band of *Cahiers du Cinéma* critic-filmmakers led by François Truffaut, that virulent young critic who attacked and destroyed all the most respected and prestigious French film productions in his columns for *Arts* magazine, was there any real aesthetic coherence to the New Wave? Was it simply a phenomenon of renewal thanks to the arrival of a new generation, an event that arrives every 20 years anyway? Did it have disastrous effects by glorifying amateurish techniques and a cult of improvisation at the expense of solid scripts, basing a film's quality on perceptions of a few directors and critics? Did it chase average spectators from the theaters? Is it not true that these films appeared at the very moment when the curve for movie attendance began its dizzying descent, which cut audiences in half? Finally, why has this myth survived for so long since the 1960s? And, why did Jean-Luc Godard use this famous expression, "*La Nouvelle Vague*," as the name of his 1990 film, featuring the popular actor Alain Delon, 30 years after his own "Nouvelle Vague" triumph, *A bout de souffle* (*Breathless*, 1960)?

Nearly every year, on the occasion of some film festival or in the summary of the year's trends in film production, chroniclers ask whether there are any signs of another "New Wave" on the horizon. Whenever two young directors display some evidence of complicity, someone sees in them the potential nucleus of a group that will create a movement of thematic or aesthetic renewal along the model established by this mythical and now distant New Wave. In nature, the movement of waves may repeat endlessly with the rhythm of the seas, but in French cinema, the wave of 1959 remains unique. It is that singularity which this book strives to demonstrate by providing some answers to the questions posed above.

The New Wave is indeed a victim of its own fame, and yet it is difficult to cite a single work within the last twenty years that carefully analyzes this phenomenon.[1] James Monaco's *The New Wave*, published in 1976, has been out of print for years, and was more of an auteurist summary than an historical investigation. Jean-Luc Douin edited a book in 1983, *La Nouvelle Vague vingt-cinq ans après* (*The New Wave, 25 Years Later*), which offered a number of observations and picturesque reflections, but it is a study that remains very limited.[2] In short, most beginning film students and film buffs believe they already know everything about the movement, but this knowledge is often limited to several common sources or short summaries in survey histories that do not always stand up to the test of historical evaluation.

My hypothesis will be the following: the French New Wave was a coherent movement, which existed for a limited period of time, and whose emergence was favored by a series of simultaneous factors intervening at the close of the 1950s, and especially during 1958–9. I will describe these various factors in the first three chapters. I will also propose a fairly strict definition of the concept of a *school* in film history. The New Wave was, first of all, a journalistic slogan connected with a critical movement, that of the "Hitchcocko-Hawksians," as they were rather ironically labeled by film critic and theorist André Bazin, co-founder of *Cahiers du Cinéma*. I will privilege here, however, an analysis organized around the economic and technical trends surrounding the appearance of these films, giving comparatively less attention to thematic and stylistic factors. This focus of inquiry fits recent tendencies in cinema history which strive to give a privileged place to economic and technical mechanisms in order to anchor more fully aesthetic observations in their generating conditions, which include the production and distribution of films, their commercial fate, and, also, the political and cultural context of this era in France. I have included a chronology of major political and cultural events in the Appendix to help give a concise overview of the era.

This book does not offer detailed analyses of individual films. Rather, it makes every effort to present a global synthesis of a movement distinguished by both strengths and weaknesses. Readers of this book could obviously benefit from seeing or re-seeing key films cited here, as well as consultation of critical studies of particular films. For instance, recent studies by Anne Gillain, Carole Le Berre, Jean-Louis Leutrat, and myself, devoted to *Les 400 coups* (*The 400 Blows*, Truffaut, 1959), *Jules et Jim* (*Jules and Jim*, Truffaut, 1961), *Hiroshima mon amour* (*Hiroshima My Love*, Resnais, 1959), and *Le Mépris* (*Contempt*, Godard, 1963), as well as Michel Cieutat on *Pierrot le fou* (Godard, 1965), Dudley Andrew on *Breathless*, and Barthélemy Amengual on *Bande à part* (*Band of Outsiders*, 1964), are all very useful.[3] For a larger overview of the historical period, one could consult the following books. In French, René Prédal's *Cinquante ans de cinéma français* is a helpful encyclopedic text that should be useful for young *cinéphiles* today,[4] while Jacques Siclier's synthetic *Le Cinéma français*, volumes I and II, or Jean-Michel Frodon's *L'Age moderne du cinéma français* are equally important.[5] In English, general sources include Alan Williams's *Republic of Images*, Susan Hayward's *French National Cinema*, and the reference book *The Companion to French Cinema* by Ginette Vincendeau.[6] Many of these books cover the lively period from the French liberation to the New Wave and beyond.

Michel Marie would like to thank the following for their careful readings and critically inspired comments: Jacques Aumont, Michel Chion, Claire Hennaut, Amandine Moulette, Frédérique Moreau, Catherine Schapira, Maxine Scheinfeigel, Geneviève Sellier, and Francis Vanoye. He especially thanks Françoise Juhel for her patience. Richard Neupert is indebted to Michel Marie for the opportunity to translate *La Nouvelle Vague*. Michel has been a terrific and inspiring teacher as well. Jayne Fargnoli, Sarah Dancy and the editorial staff at Blackwell Publishers have been delightful to work with and truly dedicated to getting this translation published. Finally, the other person who has been most essential for the English-language version of *The French New Wave: An Artistic School* is Catherine M. Jones. Her constant, invaluable assistance enriched the translation and made it proceed quickly, smoothly, and correctly. She should really be listed as co-translator.

Chapter One
A Journalistic Slogan and a New Generation

L'Express and their "New" Campaign

S URPRISINGLY, THE EXPRESSION "NOUVELLE VAGUE," which refers for everyone today to a moment in French film history and a particular collection of films, such as *The 400 Blows* and *Breathless*, was not specifically linked to cinema at the beginning. The label appeared in a sociological investigation of the phenomenon of the new postwar generation, and the inquiry was launched and popularized by a series of articles written by Françoise Giroud for the weekly magazine *L'Express* (which is the French equivalent of *Time* or *Newsweek*). This detail of origins is important. Its genesis signals the thematic role played by the new youthful generation, but also the role played during the 1950s by a new sort of publication, represented by *L'Express*, which first appeared in 1953. We see here the beginning of a general application of surveys and inquiries as well as a particular mode of sociological studies.

In August 1957, *L'Express*, modeling itself on the American weekly news magazines, launched a huge survey, in an obvious effort to reach and define its new readership. With the collaboration of the Institut français d'opinion publique (IFOP), they tried to question nearly eight million French people between the ages of 18 and 30, a segment of the population who, in ten years, "will have taken France in hand, their elders taking leave, the younger ones helping move them out."[1] The theme of "the succession of generations," crucial, as we will see, in regard to the cinema, was already strongly present in the ideological landscape in the late 1950s. France would change its face, its government, and also its cinema. The survey's results appeared in *L'Express* between October 3 and December 12, 1957 with the slogan "The New Wave Arrives!" and an accompanying photograph of a smiling young woman. The tallies also reappeared in a volume published by Françoise Giroud under the title *La Nouvelle Vague: portraits de la jeunesse* (*The New Wave: Portraits of Youth*). Within these portraits, the researchers touched on all subjects: clothing habits, morals, values, lifestyles, and cultural behavior, amongst which the cinema was of secondary importance. When films are mentioned, they are titles said to parallel this "new generation's" values, and are summarized by the researchers as representing "new moral values, presented with refreshing, never before seen frankness."

It is not difficult to imagine how Roger Vadim's first feature, *Et Dieu créa la femme* (*And God Created Woman*), which premiered in Paris on November 28, 1956, became the exemplary, "call to arms" film for this mindset. His leading actress, Brigitte Bardot, who was just 22 years old, symbolized the young French woman who was finally "free and liberated." Vadim, who had been a young journalist for *Paris-Match* magazine, and assistant director and screenwriter for fairly traditional films, such as Marc Allégret's *Futures Vedettes* (*Future Stars*, 1955) and Michel Boisrond's *Cette Sacrée Gamine* (*That Naughty Girl*, 1955), knew what he was doing in selecting such a title. The press responded: "Vadim's cinema creates a new image of the young French woman," and that image was suddenly much more exportable than the established typical 1950s French woman as portrayed by Martine Carol, Michèle Morgan, or Françoise Arnoul. We will return later to the image offered by this new sort of French girl proposed by Vadim's film. But first it is important to underline the revealing role played by a social phenomenon: huge numbers of young French women identified with the character Juliette in *And God Created Woman*, and even more with the actress who incarnated her, Brigitte Bardot, as scholar Françoise Audé has explained in her 1981 book, *Ciné-modèles, cinéma d'elles*."[2]

In 1959, during the early furor over the New Wave, a journalist asked François Truffaut, "Does the label 'New Wave' correspond to reality?" Truffaut responded:

Bardot as Juliette, "the new French woman;" *And God Created Woman* (Vadim, 1956).
Produced by Raoul J. Levy

I think the New Wave had an anticipated reality. It was, after all, first an invention by journalists, which became a reality. In any case, even if no one had invented this journalistic slogan at the Cannes Film Festival, I think the label, or some other, would have been created by the force of events as people became aware of the number of "first films" coming out.

The "New Wave" originally designated a real, official survey carried out in France by some statistical research agency on French youth in general. The "New Wave" was about future doctors, future engineers, future lawyers. That

7

study was published in *L'Express*, which lent it broad public attention, and for a number of weeks *L'Express* appeared with the sub-title "*L'Express*, the magazine of the New Wave" on the front page.[3]

From the Perspective of Critical Cinema Journals

The journal *Cinéma*, published by the French Federation of *Ciné-clubs* and edited by Pierre Billard, first appeared in November 1954, at the very moment when nationalistic movements set in motion what would become the Algerian War. The first issue of *Cinéma 54* (the title changed with each new year) featured a cover photo of actor Gérard Philipe holding actress Danielle Darrieux in his arms, from a publicity still for *Le Rouge et le noir* (*The Red and the Black*, Claude Autant-Lara, 1954). Autant-Lara's film was very representative of the dominant aesthetic known as the "tradition of quality" at the heart of a certain tendency of French film production.

Four years later, in February 1958, Pierre Billard proposed an inquiry into the younger generation of French cinema. The specialized press thus followed the example set by the new weekly magazines. The report was entitled, "40 who are under 40: The young academy of French cinema." While the front cover of this small journal featured a standard publicity portrait of Ava Gardner in *The Sun Also Rises* (Henry King, 1957), the back cover was devoted to two very different photos: one was Brigitte Bardot (apparently naked, hiding behind two fans), the second was a popular, 30-year-old actor named Darry Cowl, and the caption read, "The two favorite muses of the young academy of French cinema."

Pierre Billard applied one strict biographical criterion, the date of a person's birth, in distinguishing between "*ancien*" (a word suggesting both older and ancient) directors born before 1914, and "new" directors born after 1918. This dividing line left Jean-Pierre Melville, born in 1917, to fall between the cracks, since he was older than the young generation, but also an important precursor of their movement, as he himself attested on numerous occasions. It was the notion, however, of a "young academy" or school that recurred systematically during the article, while the term "New Wave" was used only once as a detour in a paragraph to designate clearly some unsettling, observed conformism: "The prudence with which this New Wave follows in the steps of their elders is disconcerting." Admittedly, when Billard wrote this in February 1958, Claude Chabrol had just finished *Le Beau Serge*, shot during December 1957 and January 1958. But *Le Beau Serge* would not be released for a full year, premiering on February 11, 1959 at the Studio Publicis in Paris, so Billard's notion of a young academy seems a bit premature to us now.

It was again *L'Express* that renewed the New Wave label by applying it to new films distributed early in 1959, and in particular to the youthful works presented at the Cannes Film Festival that spring. This time, the original generational and social senses of the term were swept away so that it could be employed more strictly in relation to the cinema, and this specialized focus was in part due to the extraordinary success of a publicity campaign orchestrated by Unifrance-film, the official agency of the Centre national de la cinématographie (CNC) charged with promoting French film abroad. Their activity intervened directly on the heels of the 1959 Cannes Film Festival, which had been organized for the first time under the tutelage of the new Minister of Culture, André Malraux, who was both a famous novelist and a filmmaker. The term "New Wave" was quickly relayed by the daily and weekly press and was unfurled from their columns during the entire film season between spring 1959 and spring 1960. Truffaut's interview confirms the importance of this festival:

> Because of this stroke of luck, which turned the Festival into a forum for films by young directors – not just for France, but also for foreign nations – the film reviewers and journalists made use of this expression to designate a certain group of young directors who did not necessarily come from among critics, since Alain Resnais and Marcel Camus were included. And that is how this slogan was forged. In my opinion, it never really corresponded to reality in the sense that, for example, outside of France, in particular, people seemed to believe there was an association of young French directors who got together regularly and had a plan, a common aesthetic, when in fact there was never anything like that and it was all a fiction, made up from those outside.[4]

The Colloquium at La Napoule

In tandem with the Cannes Festival, Unifrance-film took the initiative to assemble some young and even future directors at La Napoule, a few miles from the central Croisette of Cannes, for a colloquium sponsored by the Minister of Culture, with Georges Altman standing in for André Malraux. It very directly demonstrated to a number of foreign journalists already present at what was a very media-hyped Festival that a changing of the guard was at work within the French film industry.

A large number of critics, as well as the famous critic-directors from *Cahiers du Cinéma*, participated in debates organized by *Cahiers* editor Jacques Doniol-Valcroze and featuring Truffaut, Chabrol, and Jean-Luc Godard. Other directors present included Roger Vadim, Robert Hossein, who had directed *Les Salauds vont en enfer* (*Bastards Go to Hell*, 1955) and *Pardonnez nos offenses* (*Forgive Us Our Sins*, 1956), Edouard Molinaro, François Reichenbach, Edmond Séchan, Jean-Daniel Pollet, Marcel Camus, Jean Valère, and Louis Félix. The proceedings from this colloquium were immediately published by the weekly journal *Arts*, the regular home to Truffaut's critical articles, under the title, "For the First Time, at the La Napoule Colloquium, the New French Cinema Defines its Statement of Policies."[5]

Of course, any analysis of these presentations reveals that there was no set definition, but, rather, deeply divided opinions. With great enthusiasm and ingeniousness, Robert Hossein, followed by Edouard Molinaro and Marcel Camus, proposed organizing a "constituent assembly of young cinema," which anticipated by ten years the "States General" proposed for cinema during the strikes at Cannes in May and June 1968. Chabrol, Truffaut, and Doniol-Valcroze politely approved of the idea, but refused the concrete measures proposed by the rash idealism of Hossein. Louis Malle and Jean-Luc Godard put forth very polemical arguments, undercutting any unanimous front, with Godard serving as a killjoy for the assembly even though he had so far only shot several virtually unknown short films. Nonetheless, publication of these debates jump-started anew the media campaign surrounding all the new young filmmakers in France.

The serious daily newspaper *Le Monde*, which at the time was very circumspect with regard to these cinematic developments, published a series of interviews with directors of all ages in August 1959. They included patriarchs such as Jean Renoir and René Clair as well as newcomers Louis Malle and Alexandre Astruc, while Roger Vadim and Georges Franju represented the intermediate generation. *Le Monde* also asked Raoul Lévy, producer of *And God Created Woman*, "Does a New Wave really exist?" Lévy replied, "I think the New Wave is just a huge joke." Following *L'Express* and *Le Monde*'s lead, *France Observateur* had Pierre Billard organize two round tables. The first, late in 1959, included Truffaut, Doniol-Valcroze, Jacques Rivette, and Pierre Kast. The second, in October 1960, involved Truffaut, Eric Rohmer, Godard, and Marcel Moussy. This very selective list demonstrates that it was above all the critic-directors from *Cahiers du Cinéma* who occupied the microphones, much to the rancor of the older generation, from Claude Autant-Lara to René Clément, who were admittedly less garrulous, but also much less sought out by the media. Finally, it would be vain to try to search through the testimony from this era hoping to isolate a single coherent definition of the movement, especially in light of the debate published in 1960 that concluded by stating, "The New Wave is diversity itself."

This promotional process really found its most assured cultural consecration in the publication of books devoted to the movement, which were written and published with remarkable speed. The New Wave barely existed, it was elusive and undefinable, but it was already the object of historical exegesis. André-Sylvain Labarthe, collaborator at *Cahiers*, published his *Essai sur le jeune cinéma français* (*Essay on the Young French Cinema*) in Italian format by June 1960.[6] Jacques Siclier followed the rapid trend with a small book, prudently entitled *Nouvelle Vague?* Written between September 1959 and December 1960, Siclier's book first appeared in February 1961, in the celebrated "7th Art" series published by Cerf, which had also just published the four-volume, complete works of *Cahiers*' founder and master critic André Bazin, *What is Cinema?*

This consecration of the New Wave drew polemical attacks as well. Rebuttal began quickly once Raymond Borde, Freddy Buache, and Jean Curtelin united to publish an extraordinarily vicious pamphlet against the

11

movement. Their argument, partly published as articles in 1959 and 1960, was based on the critical positions of *Positif*, a rival French film journal, opposed to *Cahiers*, and its militant, ideological committment.[7] Their booklet tried to present itself as a sort of assessment of what they saw as the New Wave's deception, combined with its obituary:

> Certain beginners have thrown themselves into directing, much like young girls in the nineteenth century used to paint watercolors in order to occupy their gilded leisure time. These directors will disappear rather quickly. Others have a career in mind, and since teaching did not pay enough or management school was too difficult, they took the path that led to the studios, intending to remain there. Their little "message," as the undertakers of culture say, was delivered right away: it was generally an inane moral principle for adults, occasionally mixed with a libertine crisis of originality. Next they dropped anchor and here they are, I do believe, moored in the profession. This is the case with Claude Chabrol, François Truffaut, Edouard Molinaro, Robert Hossein, Louis Malle, and Jacques Doniol-Valcroze. We have not seen the last of their names on the credits, and, if they know how to swim, they have before them the same future as their elders: Christian-Jacque, Léo Joannon, and Jean Delannoy.[8]

Birthdate: February–March 1959

In an effort to mark the boundaries of the terrain with a bit of precision and avoid any uncontrollable expansion of this historical movement, which risks including precursors like *Le Silence de la mer* (*Silence of the Sea*, Jean-Pierre Melville, 1948) or post-New Wave films like *Weekend* (Godard, 1967), or even Godard's later film entitled *La Nouvelle Vague*, we have to impose a few limits. As I have explained, the expression "New Wave" appeared and then came into systematic use within the popular press in February and March of 1959. The term initially accompanied the commercial release of Claude Chabrol's two features, *Le Beau Serge* and *The Cousins*. The release of these two features followed one after the other because the former had remained in the can for nearly a year. But, just as Godard began to shoot *Le Mepris* (*Contempt*, 1964) before *Les Carabiniers* (*The Soldiers*, 1963) had been released, Chabrol shot his second feature *before* the release of his first, thanks in part to the "Quality Aid" he received for the first (a point I will return to in the first section of chapter 3).

The New Wave's starting point (at least from the perspective of its arrival in the media): *Le Beau Serge*, filmed between December 1957 and January 1958; premiere, February 11, 1959; and *The Cousins*, filmed during July and August 1958; premiere, March 11, 1959.

This double release of Chabrol's films was followed two months later, in May 1959, by the very unexpected selection of François Truffaut's *The 400 Blows* to represent France at the Cannes Film Festival, along with Marcel Camus' *Orphée noir* (*Black Orpheus*). Truffaut won the Best Director Award and Camus won the Palme d'Or for best film. The nomination of Truffaut's film came despite very strong opposition from within the established cinema crowd, especially since Truffaut had been banned from Cannes the previous year for his vicious article attacking the French film industry, "The French Cinema Is Crushed by False Legends," published in *Arts*. (We will return to the significance of this article in the next chapter.) In addition, Culture Minister André Malraux, who was prevented, for political more than aesthetic reasons, from getting his son-in-law Alain Resnais' first feature, *Hiroshima mon amour*, included in the Official Selections at Cannes, did manage to encourage its producer, Anatole Dauman to present it at Cannes outside competition. It created a sensation.

The 400 Blows and *Hiroshima mon amour* were distributed in June 1959, immediately after the Cannes Film Festival, in order to take full advantage of the journalistic and promotional bounce they had just received. Truffaut's movie opened on June 3 and Resnais' on the 10th. Their commercial success surpassed all expectations. Nevertheless, the high point for the exhibition of New Wave films arrived the next spring with the release of *Breathless* by Godard, which sold 259,000 tickets in its Paris first run, beginning in March 1960. In the meantime, Claude Chabrol's third feature, *À double tour* had been released on December 4, 1959, as well as Pierre Kast's *Le Bel Âge*, on February 10, 1960. But during 1960 there were already commercial and media reactions against the New Wave phenomenon: Chabrol's fourth feature, *Les Bonnes Femmes* (*The Good Girls*), released on

13

April 22, was a critical and financial failure. In addition, Jacques Rivette's first feature, *Paris nous appartient* (*Paris Belongs to Us*) as well as Eric Rohmer's *Le Signe du Leo* (*Sign of the Lion*) found no commercial distribution and would have to wait three years to be shown, and then only in limited releases. Even more serious was the total banning of Godard's second feature, *Le Petit Soldat*, in the spring of 1960. Because of its references to torture and the Algerian War, it could not be shown in France until 1963. Godard's third feature, *Une Femme est une femme* (*A Woman is a Woman*, 1961), was also a commercial failure, as was Truffaut's second, *Tirez sur le pianiste* (*Shoot the Piano Player*, 1960).

In short, especially from the media's official perspective, the New Wave really only marked two seasons of French cinema, from the beginning of 1959 to the end of 1960. From that point on the films received uneven receptions both from the public and the critics. As we will see in chapter 2, even directors who were themselves an integral part of the movement, such as François Truffaut and Jean-Luc Godard, initially denounced what they saw as an erroneous label, lumping together such a wide range of films from young directors. They argued instead that each was distinct and not part of any group style. Later, however, as the New Wave aesthetic came under vicious attack from some critics as well as many older directors, and especially those from the so-called "Tradition of Quality" and mainstream popular cinema, these young individualist directors radically changed their strategies and affirmed their membership in the New Wave movement, while defending the originality of its collective aesthetic choices.

It is even more risky to try to propose a date to mark the end of the movement than it is to find its beginning. As mentioned, the end of 1960 did mark the point where negative criticism and financial failures increased. And, while 1957 marked the peak of movie attendance in France, with 411 million spectators, 1958 proved the beginning of the drop in attendance that would continue for a decade. There was a decline from 354 million tickets sold in 1959 to 328 million in 1961 and only 292 million in 1963. From 1957 to 1969 the crisis in attendance became dizzying, ending with 184 million tickets sold at the end of the decade. The French cinema had lost one half its audience in only 15 years.[9] This phenomenon was not limited to France, since the British and German industries were affected as well during these years, but there were many critics in France who could not restrain themselves from laying blame for the decline on the appearance of so many films by young directors. The New Wave was painted as the villain.

While *The 400 Blows* and *Breathless* each attracted as many as 450,000 spectators by the end of their first showings throughout France, *Shoot the Piano Player* sold 70,000 tickets, *A Woman is a Woman* 65,000, Chabrol's *Les Godelureaux* (*Wise Guys*, 1960) 23,000, and Jacques Demy's first feature, the amazing *Lola* (1961), only 35,000 people. In response to these declines, Truffaut charged: "It is becoming clear that films by young directors, as soon as they distance themselves even slightly from the norms, immediately run up against a roadblock set up by the exhibitors and the press." He even pointed out a certain revenge by the "old wave," which was seeing many of their own films gaining great success at the box office. For instance, Jean Delannoy's *Le Baron de l'écluse* (*The Baron*, 1961), starring veteran actor Jean Gabin, sold 366,000 tickets, while Henri-Georges Clouzot's *La Vérité* (*The Truth*, 1960), featuring the young Brigitte Bardot alongside such old standbys as Charles Vanel and Paul Meurisse, was the top French film, with 527,000 sales. Another Gabin movie, written by old-guard scriptwriter Michel Audiard, *Rue des prairies* (*Rue de Paris*, 1960), was launched with one of the most explicit advertising slogans of the era: "Jean Gabin gets even with the New Wave."

However, the New Wave did not disappear so fast. The phenomenon of renewal via young directors continued until at least 160 new filmmakers had made their first features between January 1959 and the end of 1962. *Cahiers du Cinéma* published a dictionary in their December 1962 issue listing all the new directors. Claude Chabrol completed seven features in four years, but their box office returns dropped in a dramatic decline down to 84,000 tickets sold for *Les Bonnes Femmes* (*The Good Girls*, 1960), 8,000 for *L'Oeil du malin* (*The Third Lover*, 1962), and just 6,900 for *Ophélia* (1962). After the mediocre reception of *Shoot the Piano Player*, Truffaut had more luck with *Jules and Jim*, attracting 210,000 spectators. Godard too rebounded, with 148,000 tickets sold in France for *Vivre sa vie* (*My Life to Live*, 1962), before suffering another failure with *Les Carabiniers* (*The Soldiers*, 1963) which only ran for two weeks and sold 2,800 tickets. This was perhaps the worst showing for any New Wave film. At the same time, Chabrol accepted an offer to shoot a commercial production, *Landru* (*Bluebeard*, 1962) in order to revive his career. This movie was based on the true story of a French serial murderer, from a script by popular novelist Françoise Sagan, and starring the established actress Michèle Morgan. Truffaut, meanwhile, struggled desperately to find funding for his next production, *Fahrenheit 451*, which he would only manage to shoot three years later. Thus, the beginning of 1963 marked a turning point: it was the beginning of the end of the New Wave era.

The New Wave had lasted only four or five years, which is by no means insignificant for a cinematic movement subject to the changing moods of the media and the inconsistent desires of the movie-going public. Despite its brief duration, however, the New Wave completely altered France's cinematic landscape, provoking a number of psychological "shocks" felt across the world, as national cinemas discovered these films and greeted them with a mixture of amazement and discomfort.

A Rather Morose "Young Academy"

At the start of 1958, Pierre Billard, editor of the journal *Cinéma 58*, published his annual appraisal of the French film industry, and his account was particularly gloomy. His summary follows the path set by *Cahiers du Cinéma*, which had registered its own disappointment with recent French cinema six months earlier in a special issue entitled "The Situation of French Cinema," (#71, May 1957), to which we will return in the next chapter. Billard's editorial pointed out that the undeniable economic prosperity of contemporary French cinema was accompanied by a deep artistic crisis: "It is hard to disagree that inspirations have run dry, subject-matters are sterile, and film aesthetics ever more static. With a few rare exceptions, the best films in recent years come from outdated conceptions of form and content."[10] Billard calls attention to "hopefuls who have already disappointed or are still to be proven," listing a number of directors to watch: Edouard Molinaro, "auteur of short films full of humor," who was just beginning to shoot his first feature, *Le Dos au mur* (*Back to the Wall*, 1958) based on the novel by Frédéric Dard; Roger Pigaud, who had just filmed *Le Cerf-volant du bout du monde* (*The Kite That Flew to the End of the Earth*, 1957) in France and China; Robert Ménégoz, auteur of a short film getting a great deal of attention, *Vivent les dockers* (*Life of Dockers*, 1957), and had recently begun shooting *The Great Wall* in China, which was never completed. Finally, Billard cited "the talented Louis Malle," co-director along with Jacques Cousteau of *Le Monde du silence* (*The Silent World*, 1956), and more recently, winner of the Louis Delluc Award for his own first feature, *L'Ascenseur pour l'échafaud* (*Elevator to the Gallows*, 1957).

Pierre Billard's second category, helping rank the forty most interesting directors under the age of 40, was entitled "False and Real Greats." This group includes Yves Ciampi, Henri Verneuil, Denys de la Patellière, Jack Pinoteau, Hervé Bromberger, Claude Boissol, Michel Boisrond, Charles Brabant, Norbert Carbonnaux, Robert Hossein, Marcel Camus, and Alex Jaffé. Billard also mentions Alexandre Astruc for his *Les Mauvaises Rencontres* (*Bad Encounters*, 1955), which he somewhat devalues, criticizing its excessive formalism. By contrast, he overvalues Roger Vadim's first feature, *And God Created Woman*. But, in praising it, Billard followed the reactions of most of his critic colleagues at the time, all of whom were captivated by Vadim's modernity:

> What style! Vadim has successfully managed to create personal and endearing films with Curt Jurgens, the Côte d'Azur, and Brigitte Bardot in *And God Created Woman*, and again in Venice even with an infantile story to adapt in *Sait-on jamais?* (*No Sun in Venice*, 1957). He likes jazz, money, pretty girls, and publicity . . . like you and I. He is thus very modern. [We must certainly ponder here Billard's definition of modernity.] He knows how to create probable story situations that overturn conventions, as well as retorts that set him apart from Henri Jeanson. His number one quality: classy nonchalance. His principal fault: being a dilettante. I would gladly put my money on his success at a 50:1 shot, if I were convinced he would not end up a producer, corporate head, professor at the University of Alabama, or Minister of the Navy.[11]

Next, Billard has no trouble contrasting the pallor of this new academy of French cinema with the revelations marking a renewal among international filmmakers during the mid-1950s: Robert Aldrich in the USA had just made *Kiss Me Deadly* and *The Big Knife*, both released in 1955, the Soviet Union's Grigori Chukhrai directed *The Forty-First* (1956), Spain's Juan Antonio Bardem made *Death of a Cyclist* (1955) and *Main Street* (1956), while Poland's André Wajda caught attention with *A Girl Talked* (1955) and *Kanal* (1956), and Italy's Francesco Maselli directed *The Doll That Took the Town* (1956). Billard attributes the comparative weakness of France's overall cinematic sphere, which was "very unfavorable to the new generation's attempts to take flight," to the following problems:

- the absence of a strong sector for experimental film production;
- the absurdity and incoherence of the profession's organization, which creates multiple barriers and dividers between various specialties, and reinforces strict hierarchies among jobs;
- relative prosperity within the realm of short filmmaking, which retains some of the best talent;
- a tendency in French production to develop "big international films" co-produced with other countries, featuring foreign stars, in color, with high budgets, and which are thus offered to established directors who have already proven themselves, at least commercially, with similar projects;
- finally, a lack of any real spirit for experimentation or risky ventures on the part of producers who offer most of their work to a small number of directors "who are work horses but without talent."

During 12 years, from 1945 to 1957, *167 films*, or 20 percent of France's total production output, were shot by only *9 directors*, for an average of 18 movies each. It is worth listing all their names so as to perceive better the true nature of French cinema during the 1950s. These are the filmmakers who were supported by producers and to whose movies most of the cinema-going public flocked: André Berthomieu (30 films), Jean Stelli (22 films), Jean Boyer (21 films), Richard Pottier (18 films), Robert Vernay and Maurice Labro (17 films each), Henri Lepage, Maurice de Canonge, and Raoul André (14 films each). These directors were all professionals who shared a narrowly artisanal conception of their work. They directed their films so as to maximize their box office takings and thus increase the return on production costs. A complete list of their films would be excessive here, but, needless to say, this state of affairs was not able to permit a renewal of creativity such as could be seen in the ongoing revival of 1950s French literature and theater.

Pierre Billard concluded his essay by warning that new talent was moving over into television or reinforcing the brilliant successes in the area of short film production. He wondered also about the semi-abandoned effort by Jacques Rivette, *Le Coup du berger* (*Fool's Mate*, 1956), and the semi-success of François Truffaut's *Les Mistons* (*The Mischief Makers*, 1957), while also calling attention to Claude Chabrol's upcoming feature, *Le Beau Serge* (1958), as well as a number of other short and feature-length projects in the works "from those at *Cahiers du Cinéma* now undertaking independent productions. Could these projects have a chance of success at creating interesting revelations?" His suggestion certainly proved insightful.

French Cinema in 1958: The State of Affairs

Aesthetic sclerosis and good economic health: this summary reflects French cinema just before the explosion that was to be the New Wave. The ten years separating 1947 and 1957 were bracketed by two years of record high box office attendance, with 423 million tickets sold in 1947, and 411 million in 1957. During this period, 1952 was the lowest, with 359 million movie-goers. The French went regularly to the cinema, especially for Saturday night shows. In that way, the 1950s proved to be a continuation of the high attendance numbers of the Occupation years of the early 1940s, making exhibitors quite prosperous. Hence the myth of a new "Golden Age of French Cinema" during the reign of Maréchal, with "gold" taking on a purely monetary sense here, at least for distributors and theater owners.

The number of films produced each year averaged between 120 and 140, with 129 in 1956, 142 in 1957, and 126 in 1958. That range corresponds fairly closely to the market capacity, and there was now none of the over-production that had been seen during some of the prewar years in France.

For instance, during 1933 there were 143 movies made plus 32 French versions of films made outside France. The only weak wing in the 1950s was the export market, where, other than in the French colonies and territories, French films were having a tough time competing with American movies. If Vadim's *And God Created Woman* became a mythical film so rapidly, it was in part due to its unexpected success abroad, especially on British, Brazilian, German, and North American screens, following a respectable but hardly record-breaking first run in France. This phenomenon of highly successful international distribution would recur with the first films of the New Wave, such as *The 400 Blows, Breathless*, and *Hiroshima mon amour*.

As for the popular audience in France, the films attended most during the second half of the 1950s were big budget American movies, including *War and Peace* (Vidor, 1956), *Around the World in 80 Days* (Anderson, 1957), followed by England's *Bridge on the River Kwai* (Lean, 1957), as well as huge spectacle blockbusters, whose prototype was Cecil B. DeMille's *Ten Commandments* (1956), which was seen by 526,000 people in its Parisian first run alone. But French comedies were also very popular, including Jack Pinoteau's *Le Triporteur* (*The Tricyclist*), starring Darry Cowl, which was the third-biggest money-maker of 1957, followed by Jean Dréville's *A pied, à cheval, et en spoutnik* (*A Dog, A Mouse, and Sputnik*, 1958). French detective films, or *policiers*, were also successful, especially the semi-parodic *Les Femmes s'en balancent* (*The Women Couldn't Care Less*, Borderie, 1954) and *Votre dévoué Blake* (*Your Man Blake*, Laviron, 1954), both of which helped launch Eddie Constantine as a star.

Another film, directed by a young auteur, became a huge success: Louis Malle's second feature, *Les Amants* (*The Lovers*, 1958). Its high returns were undoubtedly fueled by the bold presentation of the sexual relations between the central characters, played by Jeanne Moreau and Jean-Marc Bory. The staging of these scenes was quite daring for the era, and *The Lovers* transformed Moreau into an international star.[12]

Other French successes of the mid-1950s were achieved by veteran director Sacha Guitry, whose *Si Versailles m'était conté* (*Royal Affairs in Versailles*) was the top film of 1954, selling 685,000 tickets, and Henri-Georges Clouzot, whose *Les Diaboliques* followed Guitry to the top in 1955.

In addition, René Clair's *Les Grandes Manoeuvres* (*The Grand Maneuver*) came in fourth at the box office in 1955. During 1956, three French films came in behind Vidor's *War and Peace*: Jean Delannoy's *Notre-Dame de Paris* (*Hunchback of Notre Dame*), René Clément's *Gervaise*, and Claude Autant-Lara's *La Traversée de Paris* (*Four Bags Full / Pigs Over Paris*).

In 1958, Marcel Carné saw his first real triumph since 1945's *Les Enfants du Paradis* (*Children of Paradise*), with *Les Tricheurs* (*The Cheats*), while Jacques Tati was also very successful with *Mon Oncle* and Denys de La Patellière scored big with *Les Grandes Familles* (*The Possessors*). Finally, during 1959, the year of the New Wave, the box office champion was Roger Vadim's *Liaisons dangereuses, 1960* (*Dangerous Liaisons, 1960*), followed by Marcel Camus' *Black Orpheus* and Henri Verneuil's *La Vache et le Prisonnier* (*The Cow and I*), which began its amazing long-term success story, attracting 401,000 spectators in its first run, but eventually selling more than 8,800,000 tickets in revivals over the next several decades.

Not all these successful French films were mediocre, although Dréville's *A Dog, A Mouse, and Sputnik* hardly advanced the history of cinematic art. During this period there definitely was a correspondence between the tastes of the bulk of the audience and the "tradition of quality," despite François Truffaut's vehement attacks against the latter. The excellent financial returns for *Les Diaboliques*, *Gervaise*, *The Grand Maneuver*, *Les Portes des Lilas* (*Gates of Paris*, Clair, 1957), and *The Cheats* attest to their popular appeal. These purely commercial successes must be supplemented by the panorama of "prestige films," accorded value by institutional criteria; these were French films that earned recognition at international film festivals or that garnered domestic awards, such as the critics' Louis Delluc Award, or the profession's Grand Prix of French Cinema Awards.

If, during the years 1954 through 1958, the Cannes Film Festival granted only one Palme d'Or to a French Film, Louis Malle and Jacques Cousteau's *The Silent World* in 1956, the festival nonetheless awarded prizes for directing and acting to a number of French productions: *Monsieur Ripois* (René Clément) and *Avant le déluge* (*Before the Deluge*, André Cayatte) both in 1954, *Le Mystère Picasso* (*The Mystery of Picasso*, Henri-Georges Clouzot) in 1956, *Un Condamné à mort s'est échappé* (*A Man Escaped*, Robert Bresson) in 1957, and *Mon Oncle* (Jacques Tati) in 1958. Then, in 1959, Marcel Camus and *Black Orpheus* were honored with the Palme d'Or, while François Truffaut earned the best directing award for *The 400 Blows*.

André Cayatte, Henri-Georges Clouzot, and René Clément, all of whom were considered "quality directors" by Truffaut, and the auteurs Robert Bresson and Jacques Tati, were all internationally recognized thanks to Cannes, which can act as a barometer of critical opinion. The French cinema's Grand Prix, following more traditional and corporate criteria, rewarded Autant-Lara's *Le Blé en herbe* (*The Game of Love*) in 1954, Jean-Paul Le Chanois' *Les Evadés* (*The Runaways*) in 1955, Clair's *Gates of Paris* in 1957, and Carné's *The Cheats* in 1958. However, in 1956 they were more daring, selecting Albert Lamorisse's *Le Ballon rouge* (*The Red Balloon*) and Alain Resnais' *Nuit et brouillard* (*Night and Fog*), which would also go on to win the Prix Jean Vigo that year.

The Louis Delluc Award shifted from purely traditional selections, such as *Les Diaboliques* in 1954 and *The Grand Maneuver* in 1955, to more innovative selections, with *The Red Balloon* in 1956 and *Elevator to the Gallows*, Louis Malle's first feature, in 1957. By 1958, the Louis Delluc Award reached the height of audacity, crowning what was by professional standards a very marginal production, Jean Rouch's *Moi un noir* (*Me, a Black Man*), as winner. We will later return to the importance of this Rouch film.

During this decade, Hollywood's Oscar for Best Foreign Film was several times given to French films. René Clément won twice, first with *Au-delà des grilles* (*Beyond the Gates*, 1948) in 1950, and again for *Jeux interdits* (*Forbidden Games*) in 1952. Later, Jacques Tati won for *Mon Oncle* in 1958 and Marcel Camus inevitably won with *Black Orpheus* in 1959. Between 1948 and 1958 the tastes of the American jury clearly became more refined, since they shifted from rewarding the mediocre *Monsieur Vincent* by Maurice Cloche, to honoring Tati's distinctive *Mon Oncle*.

All the recognized, big-name auteurs were thus from the generation that got their start in the days of the silent cinema, such as René Clair, or during the time of the Occupation, including Clouzot, Jacques Becker, and André Cayatte. It is nonetheless a mistake to argue, as some have, that the French cinema was an unassailable fortress. Every year new directors appeared on the scene to shoot their first features: 8 new directors in 1946, 15 in 1947, and 21 in 1951. Only the years 1954 and 1955 were particularly weak, with 9 new directors each. Nevertheless, because of all the constraints enumerated above by Pierre Billard, most of these newcomers followed the recipes established by the commercial cinema for popular consumption. The French film industry remained rather impermeable to innovation throughout the 1950s. This stasis was denounced forcefully by the collection of critics gathered at *Cahiers du Cinéma* for their issue number 71, in May 1957, devoted to "The Situation in French Cinema," to which we will return in chapter 3.

A telling sample to represent the disappointing state of affairs can be found in the films directed in the single year of 1951. The following directors each shot a feature in 1951, 12 of which were distributed in 1952: Guy Lefranc's *Knock*, Jean Laviron's *Descendez, on vous demande* (*Come Down, Someone Wants You*), Henri Schneider's *La Grande Vie* (*The Big Life*), Henri Lavorel's *Le Voyage en Amérique* (*Voyage to America*), Claude Barma's *Le Dindon* (*The Turkey*), Jack Pinoteau's *Ils étaient cinq* (*They Were Five*), Henri Verneuil's *La Table aux crevés* (*Table for the Exhausted*), Bernard Borderie's *Les Loups chassent la nuit* (*Wolves Hunt at Night*), Daniel Gélin's *Les Dents longues* (*The Long Teeth*), André Michel's *Trois Femmes* (*Three Women*), Ralph Baum's *Nuits de Paris* (*Paris Nights*), and Georges Combret's *Musique en tête* (*Band Out Front*). The bulk of these titles never played outside France and have since been long forgotten. However, from this list, distinguished primarily for its continuation of old formulas, we might isolate *The Big Life*, Henri Schneider's only movie, which was a rather clumsy attempt at imitating neorealism, but which nonetheless earned the first-ever Jean Vigo Award. And, in addition, actor Daniel Gélin's *The Long Teeth*, which was the tale of an ambitious young journalist who leaves Lyons to come to Paris and win the job as editor-in-chief of *Paris-France*. The storyline is very similar to Alexandre Astruc's first feature, *Bad Encounters*, and *The Long Teeth* would prove to be Gélin's only feature film.

Following *The Turkey*, Claude Barma, who had participated in the filming of the Liberation of Paris in 1944, was so discouraged by the state of the film industry in the early 1950s that he switched over to the new medium of television, where he joined Pierre Dumayet and Pierre Desgraupes on the TV series "In Your Soul and Conscience," and staged *Macbeth*, *Hamlet*, and *Cyrano de Bergerac* with actor Daniel Sorano. Barma was certainly not the only young director to follow this path. Most recent graduates of the national film school, IDHEC (Institut des hautes études cinématographiques), had trouble entering the film industry and opted instead for careers in television. Some even went on to help constitute the TV documentary school at the famous Paris Buttes-Chaumont Studio. French cinema and the national television network remained shut off from one another. Transferring back and forth from one medium to the other remained quite rare, in contrast to production practices during this same period in England and the United States, where some actors, writers, directors, and other crew members could move across media.

The directors from this decade that are retained by most film histories include Jean Renoir, Robert Bresson, Max Ophuls, Jacques Tati, Jacques Becker, Jean Cocteau, and Jean Grémillon. Of these, only Grémillon was omitted by François Truffaut in his famous article, "A Certain Tendency of the French Cinema," where he listed the top auteurs, though he also included, partly as provocation, Abel Gance and his *Le Tour de Nesle* (*Tower of Nesle*, 1954), as well as Roger Leenhardt, who had shot only one movie, *Les Dernières Vacances* (*The Last Vacation*, 1947). We will return to Truffaut's controversial article in the next chapter.[13]

By 1958, the French cinema had clearly become increasingly industrial, even if film production remained, at least in strictly economic terms, somewhat artisanal. It churned out picture shows principally to entertain and turn a healthy profit. However, by the end of the decade French cinema would subtly change its social function, becoming more a means of artistic expression, in partial response to Alexandre Astruc's predictions (which I will expand upon in chapter 2). The tens of thousands of ciné-clubs that characterized French film culture in the 1950s helped contribute a great deal to this transformation. Significantly, in 1959, the cinema would leave the domain of the Ministry of Industry and Commerce for its new home within the newly formed Ministry of Culture.

The "New Wave" became one of the ways this brutal rupture of the cinema's social status was expressed. Adapting the structures for film production to new functions would take all of four decades to accomplish. It is worth noting, however, that since 1908 this sort of radical adjustment of the norms of French cinema had been regularly occurring, always labeled a "cinema crisis."

Chapter Two
A Critical Concept

A Critical School

THE NEW WAVE DIRECTORS initially and repeatedly denied that they formed a unified movement. For instance, François Truffaut proclaimed: "I see only one common point shared by young directors: we all play pinball while older directors drink scotch and play cards."[1] Despite the many denials, however, this artistic trend was closely tied to a collection of critical concepts held by a fairly coherent group. One of the first criteria for belonging to the New Wave was to have experience as a film critic. These young directors were all *cinéphiles*, or very devoted film buffs, who knew their film history inside out. They acquired their understanding of cinematic culture from watching thousands of films, gaining clear ideas about *mise-en-scène* that were based on aesthetic choices, moral options, personal tastes, and sometimes violent disapproval. But these tastes and ideas found a material form in a large number of articles, public debates, and interventions in the press, written and on the radio waves, throughout the 1950s. These future directors first found expression with pen and paper, and some, such as Jean-Luc Godard, always maintained that there was a continuity between the two practices:

> We at *Cahiers* always considered ourselves future directors. Going to ciné-clubs and the Cinémathèque was already thinking the cinema and thinking about the cinema. Writing was already making cinema because between writing and

filming there is only a quantitative difference, not a qualitative one. The only person who was completely a critic was André Bazin. The others, such as Georges Sadoul, Bela Balazs, or Pasinetti were historians or sociologists, not critics.[2]

Initially, as we saw in chapter 1, the expression "New Wave" was simply a label, as Claude Chabrol confirmed:

During 1958 and 1959, my *Cahiers* buddies and I moved into directing and were marketed like a new brand of soap. We were "la Nouvelle Vague." The expression came from Françoise Giroud, editor of *L'Express* and one of the writers most bitterly opposed to de Gaulle. She made a sort of gift of this peddler's slogan, aimed at her political adversaries of the time.[3]

Hence, "Nouvelle Vague" was first of all a journalistic slogan. But was it also an artistic movement? Or perhaps a school? The notion of a school belongs both to art history and literary history, so becomes quite pertinent here. The earliest film historians immediately transposed these handy classifications in order to establish and more easily identify trends at the beginning of the century. The transposition was made even easier because certain literary or plastic arts movements experienced continuations or resurgences in the cinema. For instance, in France, the naturalism of Emile Zola was applied to the theater by André Antoine, who trained actors and later became a filmmaker. These connections fed into the first adaptations by the Société cinématographique des auteurs and gens de lettres (SCAGL), which made *film d'art* movies influenced by theatrical and literary devices, and was allied with Pathé, resulting in productions such as *Germinal*, an adaptation of Zola's novel by Albert Capellani, in 1913. Similarly, in Germany, expressionism began as a movement in the plastic arts, then carried over into architecture, literature, and, finally, after a lag of ten years, took on a cinematic dimension, launched by the manifesto-film *The Cabinet of Dr Caligari* (Wiene, 1919).

Typically, beyond naturalism and expressionism, film scholars cite schools that include the avant-gardes of the 1920s, including the schools of Soviet montage, futurism, surrealism, and often add "realistic" schools, enumerated in all their varieties, with poetic realism, neorealism, documentary realism, socialist realism, and British "free cinema." Modern cinema, much like the so-called classical cinema, is a catch-all category with as many sub-categories as it has historical periods and nationalities. As for "postmodern" or "mannerist" cinema, their conceptual labels are even more fragile and flexible.

Despite the lack of consistency between the recognized categories, it is nonetheless valuable to refer to them, at least in order to try to define them with more precision, rather than dismiss them partially or altogether. For instance, in a chapter of his book on painting and cinema, *L'Oeil interminable*, Jacques Aumont demonstrates how fragile the notion of expressionism can be by referring to one or two titles from cinema history. Yet, chased from the hearth of rigorous theory, expressionism continued to return through the windows of critical discourse on film noir, the films of Orson Welles – especially *Citizen Kane* (1941) and *Touch of Evil* (1958) – and even Lars von Trier's *The Element of Crime* (1984).

Is the New Wave a "school?" In order to respond to this question with even a minimum of rigor, we must examine a number of parameters. A school requires many conditions:

- a body of basic critical doctrine, shared by a group of journalists or filmmakers;
- an aesthetic program, possessing some strategy;
- publication of a manifesto, explicitly announcing the doctrine;
- a group of works responding to those criteria;
- an ensemble of artists (directors, but also collaborators in creation, including writers, technicians, and actors);
- a promotional strategy and hence vehicles for diffusing that strategy, namely the press and broadcast media;
- a leader (such as the strongest personality or spokesperson of the group) and/or a theoretician (the so-called "pope" of the group) to represent the movement;
- finally, adversaries are needed, since every school defines itself at least partially in opposition to those who precede it.

It goes without saying that gathering together every one of these parameters is rarely accomplished in practice. Their degree of co-presence does determine, however, the relative solidity and coherence of any school in question. From this perspective, I will demonstrate that, contrary to the discourse by some of its own participants, the New Wave is one of the most definite and most coherent schools in film history.

In his famous *Essai sur le jeune cinéma français* (*Essay on the Young French Cinema*, 1960), André S. Labarthe provides a time-line of important events as a sort of genealogy of the movement's development. This chart took on great critical importance, and was even expanded upon two years later in the celebrated issue number 138 on the New Wave by *Cahiers du Cinéma*, whose cover featured a photo of the two female protagonists from *Adieu Philippine* (Rozier, 1962), sporting bathing suits and waving to the film's spectators and the journal's readers. The reprinting of the table in *Cahiers* may have been the first quotation, but soon nearly every history or summary of the New Wave era featured some variation on Labarthe's time-line. We reproduce it in its entirety in table 2.1.

What precisely does this list present? First, a point of departure: the year is 1948 and a critical article provided by Alexandre Astruc on the "caméra-stylo" becomes an exemplary manifesto. Astruc's essay is the first in a series of printed texts that link up with André Bazin's critical monograph on Orson Welles which also included the articles cited in *Cahiers du Cinéma* (numbers 1, 31, and 71), plus Truffaut's critical article in *Arts*. Second, a list of films is established, beginning with Varda's *La Pointe Courte*, then Vadim's *And God Created Woman*, which is included since it clearly shows the influence of American cinema and, finally, the flowering of the New Wave proper. Here, Labarthe does not cite specific titles, but his essay is founded on the analysis of *Me, a Black Man*, *Hiroshima mon amour*, *La Tête contre les murs* (*The Keepers*, Georges Franju, 1958), *Le Beau Serge*, and *Letter from Siberia* (Chris Marker, 1957). Finally, Labarthe's list specifies a club, Objectif 49, and a festival, the "anti-Cannes" of 1949: the Festival du film maudit de Biarritz (i.e. of "rejected" films).

While this genealogy can certainly be debated, it does have the strength of tradition behind it now. We will emphasize several of Labarthe's points in order to define the body of critical concepts that open an initial approach to the New Wave.

Table 2.1	New Wave time-line

1948	Alexandre Astruc publishes "La Caméra-stylo," *L'Ecran français*, no. 141.
1949	Formation of Ciné-Club "Objectif 49" and first Festival of "Films maudits," or rejected films, in Biarritz.
1950	André Bazin writes *Orson Welles*.
1951	First issue of *Cahiers du Cinéma* published.
1952	Alexandre Astruc films *Le Rideau Cramoisi* (*The Crimson Curtain*).
1954	Beginning of key critical positions established by the team at *Cahiers du Cinéma* and François Truffaut at *Arts*: *Cahiers* #31: "A Certain Tendency of the French Cinema," by François Truffaut "The Age of Directors," by Jacques Rivette "Cinemascope, End of Montage," by André Bazin.
1955	Independent film by Agnès Varda: *La Pointe Courte*.
1956	American cinema's influence is felt: *And God Created Woman* by Roger Vadim.
1957	"On the 'Politique des Auteurs'," by Bazin in *Cahiers du Cinéma*, no. 70; "Six Characters in Search of Auteurs," by André Bazin, Jacques Rivette, Jacques Doniol-Valcroze, Roger Leenhardt, and Eric Rohmer in *Cahiers*, no. 71.
1958–9	The New Wave blossoms.

Summary of key influences:
- Italian neorealism
- Documentary films
- American cinema
- Television

Alexandre Astruc's Manifesto

This text, whose full title was "The Birth of a New Avant-Garde: The Caméra-Stylo," appeared in *L'Ecran français*, issue 144, on March 30, 1948. This was far from the first article by Astruc, who had been a journalist and chronicler of literature, theater, and the cinema for most major intellectual journals of the Liberation since 1945. He had already written articles on Jean Delannoy, Henri-Georges Clouzot, André Malraux, René Clair, Robert Bresson, as well as on the crisis in contemporary French scriptwriting, and, of course, about Orson Welles, his touchstone director.

If Labarthe chose this essay by Astruc from among the thirty devoted to cinema during this period, it is because here one finds many ideas that will be returned to and largely expanded upon by François Truffaut and the *Cahiers* team. For Astruc, it was necessary to argue that cinema was in the process of becoming a new means of expression on the same level as painting and the novel:

> After having been successively a fairground attraction, an amusement analogous to boulevard theater, or a means of preserving images of an era, it is gradually becoming a language. By language, I mean a form in which and by which an artist can express his thoughts, however abstract they may be, or translate his obsessions exactly as he does in the contemporary essay or novel. This is why I would like to call this new age of cinema the age of the "*caméra-stylo*."[4]

Astruc suggests that up until 1948 the cinema had been primarily a spectacle. Previously, during the silent era, cinema was too much a prisoner to the tyranny of the visual, while, with the advent of sound, it became merely filmed theater. He affirms that there are several sorts of cinema, just as there are several sorts of literature, since, "before being an art, the cinema, just like literature, is a language that can express any aspect of thought." For him, the expression of thoughts was the fundamental challenge for the cinema, and he refers to Jacques Feyder's proposed project to adapt Montesquieu's *Spirit of Laws* and to Sergei Eisenstein's notion of adapting Karl Marx's *Capital* for the screen. These two projects would also be cited often in the wake of Astruc.

Cinema for him is defined in a strictly formal manner, as "film in movement," unfolding in time: "Every film, because its primary function is to move, i.e. to take place in time, is a theorem. It is a series of images, which, from one end to the other, have an inexorable logic (or better even, a dialectic) of their own."[5] This definition of a cinematic theorem is picked up again by Jean-Luc Godard, and again later by Pier Paolo Pasolini. Godard echoes Astruc in his review of Astruc's own feature, *Une vie* (*One Life*, 1958), from which we cite one section:

> *One Life* is a superbly constructed film. So, to illustrate my point, I shall borrow images from classical geometry. A film may be compared to a *geometrical locus*; that is, a figure constituted by all the points which satisfy a particular equation in relation to a fixed element. This ensemble of points is, if you like, the *mise-en-scène* and this particular equation common to each moment of the *mise-en-scène* will, therefore, be the scenario, or, if you prefer, the dramatic situation. There remains the fixed element, or possibly mobile one, which is none other than the theme.[6]

Back in 1948, the definition of the cinema proposed by Alexandre Astruc was at once very ambitious and quite abstract. It made no reference to the thematic content in the films discussed; thus it refused to follow the dominant critical approach of the epoch. Writing in the columns of *L'Ecran français*, the leftist journal that had grown out of the clandestine pamphlet begun during the Occupation, Astruc's claim that "between the pure cinema of the 1920s and filmed theater, there is plenty of room for a cinema that disengages," was hardly innocent in its choice of verb, since it opposed the vocabulary supporting theories of an art that *engages*, which was central to Jean-Paul Sartre and others on the editorial board at *L'Ecran*.

Astruc also took on scriptwriters and adaptations that imposed "idiotic transformations" of Balzac and Dostoevsky, reducing Balzac to a collection of images that resemble engravings emphasizing period fashions, while Dostoevsky was made to look like a popular novelist with characters who get into drinking bouts and troika races. Astruc concludes, several years before Truffaut will argue the same thing, that the scriptwriters should also direct the films themselves, because, "in this kind of filmmaking the distinction between author and director loses all meaning. Direction is no

Quote useful –

longer a means of illustrating or presenting a scene, but a true act of writing. The auteur writes with a camera as the writer writes with a pen.⁴ By its conclusion, Astruc's article has become both significant and prophetic: "These films will come, they will see the light of day." The significance of this article also lies in the fact that Astruc here offers the first affirmations of the notion of the *film auteur*, while refuting the constraints put in place by the popular cinema, which has submitted far too much to mass audiences' demands for entertainment and distraction.

Astruc's ideas hardly represented the majority opinion at *L'Ecran*, and they generated contentious arguments that lasted right up until the journal's demise in 1951. However, his views would experience a spectacular renaissance in the columns of Jean Georges Auriol's journal *Revue du cinéma* between 1946 and 1949, and again with the founding of *Cahiers du Cinéma* in 1951.

François Truffaut's Lampooning Essay

With his polemical article, "A Certain Tendency of the French Cinema," published in *Cahiers du Cinéma*, issue 31, 1954, Truffaut added a whole new dimension to Astruc's theoretical position. We know today, thanks primarily to the in-depth research by *Cahiers* historian Antoine de Baecque, that before its publication, Truffaut's essay was required to go through many revisions, primarily at the insistence of the editors-in-chief, Jacques Doniol-Valcroze and André Bazin. But their concerns clearly confirm that this article was the departure point for the auteur theory and other fundamental aesthetic positions that would become essential to the New Wave.

The editors at *Cahiers du Cinéma* had a number of reasons to harbor reservations about publishing Truffaut's essay: the polemical tone was quite vicious from such a young critic; he attacked directors who were well respected by the majority of film critics at the time, and even by some at *Cahiers*. Bazin and Doniol-Valcroze were both leftist Christians, the former a Catholic and the latter originally Protestant, and they admired the films of René Clément and some by Claude Autant-Lara. Another *Cahiers* critic,

Pierre Kast, who participated at a very young age in the French Resistance and remained deeply involved in leftist politics, was very opposed to this tract, launched by what he saw as the "hussars of the new right wing." It would be a mistake to overly simplify these political positions, which continued to evolve throughout the 1950s, but the public image of the "Hitchcocko-Hawksian" tendency within *Cahiers* was considered to belong to the conservative right. This perception played a decisive role in motivating some of the very violent attacks that the directors of the first New Wave features had to endure from the bulk of extreme left-wing and surrealist critics, which summarizes the politics at rival journal *Positif* (see reactions from Raymond Borde and Robert Benayoun below), as well as from the many various Marxist writers.

Truffaut's article is primarily a long indictment against the French cinema known as the "tradition of quality." He does not bother with run-of-the-mill commercial productions, but, rather, takes aim at a dozen or so ambitious films of the sort routinely rewarded by film festivals, movies shot by Jean Delannoy, Claude Autant-Lara, and René Clément (see chapter 1):

> These 10 or 12 films constitute what has been prettily named the "Tradition of Quality;" they force, by their ambitiousness, the admiration of the foreign press, defend the French flag twice a year at Cannes and at Venice where, since 1946, they regularly carry off medals, Golden Lions, and *grands prix* . . .
>
> The war and the postwar period renewed our cinema. It evolved under the effect of an internal pressure and for *poetic realism* – about which one might say that it died closing *Les Portes de la nuit* (*The Gates of Night*, 1946) behind it – was substituted *psychological realism*, illustrated by Claude Autant-Lara, Jean Delannoy, René Clément, Yves Allégret, and Marcel Pagliero.[7]

These "psychological realist" films were mostly literary adaptations of classic and contemporary novels, and they owed a great deal of their prestige to those original sources.

Truffaut's text was a systematic attack on the work by specific adaptation scriptwriters, the most prominent of whom were Jean Aurenche and Pierre Bost:

Today, no one is ignorant any longer of the fact that Aurenche and Bost reha-
bilitated adaptation by upsetting old preconceptions of being faithful to the letter
and substituting the contrary idea of being faithful to the spirit – to the point
that this audacious aphorism has been written: "An honest adaptation is a
betrayal" (Carlo Rim, "The Tracking Shot and Sex-Appeal").[8]

Truffaut criticizes Aurenche and Bost's practice of searching for equivalences between literary techniques and cinematic processes. In almost all
such cases, Truffaut finds a betrayal of spirit in the author's work at the
hands of a discourse specific to dialogue writers. He is most reproachful
toward adaptation scriptwriters who smuggle anarchist or anti-clerical
themes into romantic works that are very different from and far removed
from this cynical sort of world:

> You will have noticed the profound diversity of inspiration of the works and
> authors adapted. In order to accomplish this tour de force, which consists of
> remaining faithful to the spirit of Michel Davet, Gide, Fadiguet, Quefflec,
> François Boyer, Colette, and Bernanos, one must oneself possess, I imagine, a
> suppleness of spirit, a habitually geared-down personality, as well as singular
> eclecticism.[9]

Truffaut bases the proof for his argument on a comparison between the
unused adaptation script of George Bernanos' novel, *Diary of a Country
Priest*, written by Jean Aurenche, and the script that was used by Robert
Bresson for his film version in 1951. Aurenche, who adapted the novel, had
been kind enough to provide Truffaut with a copy of the script; Truffaut
found the filmed version much more faithful in rendering Bernanos' world.
To contrast them, Truffaut reveals the dialogue from a scene in Aurenche's
original script, the scene in the confessional, built around the confrontation
between the priest and Chantal, the heroine: having judged that Bernanos'
scene was "unfilmable," Aurenche substituted a sequence that reveals
Chantal telling the priest that she spit the Communion host into the missal,
or altar book. Truffaut also reproaches Aurenche for having completely
betrayed Bernanos by moving a phrase that comes in the very heart of the
novel – "When one is dead, everything is dead" – to make it the final line

of the script, even though the original novel's final line is "What does it matter? Grace is everywhere."

Truffaut thus draws several charges from his investigation of this adaptation: First, he is concerned by the infidelity to the spirit of the original, which is constant and deliberate. Second, he reveals a very strong tendency toward profanity and blasphemy. He also reproaches this anti-clerical attitude as hypocritical because the films in question are not blatantly anti-clerical, "since films about the cloth are fashionable":

> But as it suits them – they think – not to betray their convictions, the theme of profanation and blasphemy, as well as dialogues with double meanings, turn up here and there to prove to the guys that they know the art of "cheating the producer," all the while giving him satisfaction, as well as that of cheating the "great public," which is equally satisfied.[10]

For Truffaut, Aurenche and Bost are essentially literary writers and he aims his ultimate reproach at them: they show contempt for the cinema and underestimate its potential. "They behave vis-à-vis the scenario, as if they thought to reeducate a delinquent by finding him a job; they always believe they've 'done the maximum' for it by embellishing it with subtleties, out of that science of nuances that make up the slender merit of modern novels."[11] According to Truffaut, a valid adaptation can be written only by a "man of the cinema."

Theories of Adaptation

A test case

Truffaut's theses can be evaluated by comparing the first pages of the novel, *Le Diable au corps* (*Devil in the Flesh*), written by Raymond Radiguet at the end of World War I and published in 1923, with Aurenche and Bost's adaptation, filmed by Claude Autant-Lara in 1946. Truffaut refers only briefly to the contrast in his article, but it is interesting to investigate more closely any differences between the novel and the filmed version. We must also keep in mind that the movie won the Grand Prix of International Critics at the

Festival for Film and Beaux-Arts in Brussels in 1947, and it remains one of the greatest critical and popular successes of its time, the years immediately following the Liberation.

In Radiguet's short novel, written in the first person by the young narrator, the central character-narrator recounts how he met Marthe, the heroine, for the first time as she got off a train on the platform at a train station:

> When the train drew into the station, Marthe was standing on the step of the railway carriage. "Wait till it stops!" cried her mother. . . . The girl's recklessness delighted me. Her dress and hat, both simple, evidenced her lack of respect for the opinion of outsiders.[12]

Aurenche and Bost transposed the action to the courtyard of a lycée, or secondary school, transformed into a military hospital. Marthe is a volunteer aid, helping the seriously wounded soldiers arriving from the front. This change in location allows the scriptwriters to introduce a very bitter indictment against educational, military, and medical authorities, on the one hand, and against the matriarchy, on the other: the professor is a guard dog, the military doctor is a sadistic brute, and Marthe's mother-in-law is a real harpy. Thus, from these few details we can readily see how the adapters introduced via transposition a number of motifs completely absent from the original novel, whose anti-militarism, while real, was signified in a totally different, and more subtle, manner. "What is the point of this *equivalence*? It's a decoy for the anti-militarist elements added to the work by the screenwriters, in concert with Claude Autant-Lara. Well, it is evident that Radiguet's idea was one of *mise-en-scène*, whereas the scene invented by Aurenche and Bost is *literary*."[13]

Finally, Truffaut defends the idea that it is impossible to appreciate simultaneously those directors belonging to the tradition of quality, such as Autant-Lara, Jean Delannoy, René Clément, Yves Allégret, and those considered auteurs, principally Jean Renoir, Max Ophuls, Jacques Becker, and Robert Bresson, because he does not believe in the "peaceful co-existence of the *tradition of quality* and *cinema of auteurs*." The fundamental opposition established by this young critic between these two antagonistic categories rests in their directors' attitudes toward their characters: for the former, there is an all-powerful attitude in which the protagonists are only puppets manipulated by the director. "In the films of 'psychological realism' there are nothing but vile beings, but so inordinate is the authors' desire to be superior to their characters that those who, perchance, are not infamous are, at best, infinitely grotesque." By contrast, for the auteurs admired by Truffaut there is an attitude of respect shown toward the characters, an attitude illustrated by Truffaut's director, Jean Renoir, according to whom "everyone has his or her reasons":

> Well, as for these abject characters, who deliver these abject lines – I know a handful of men in France who would be incapable of conceiving them, several cinéastes whose world-view is at least as valuable as that of Aurenche and Bost, Sigurd and Jeanson. I mean Jean Renoir, Robert Bresson, Jean Cocteau, Jacques Becker, Abel Gance, Max Ophuls, Jacques Tati, Roger Leenhardt; these are, nevertheless French cinéastes and it happens – curious coincidence – that they are auteurs who often write their own dialogue and some of them invent themselves the stories they direct.[14]

A different approach toward adaptation:
Alexandre Astruc's version of Maupassant's One Life

After the commercial failure of his first feature film, *Bad Encounters*, Alexandre Astruc wrote an original script, with the help of the popular young novelist Françoise Sagan, titled *La Plaie et le couteau* (*The Wound and the Knife*). For the lead female role, Astruc thought of the actress Maria Schell, who had recently performed in *Gervaise* (1956), an adaptation of Emile Zola's novel *L'Assomoir*, directed by René Clément (but adapted by Aurenche and Bost). It was the producer of *Gervaise*, Annie Dorfmann, who, while helping Astruc secure Maria Schell for a role in his film, urged him to reread Maupassant's *One Life* and abandon his original script. These were the very conditions that, in almost caricatural fashion, determined the production of "tradition of quality" films at that time: a producer's wish, an international star, and a novelist from the nineteenth century whose works had been providing a vast reservoir of scenarios since the beginning of French films "inspired by literature." Astruc accepted the challenge and adapted Maupassant with the help of his friend Roland Laudenbach, one of the scriptwriters whom Truffaut had attacked.

However, Astruc was an auteur, a "man of cinema." He completely appropriated the initial novel, eliminating every trace of naturalism to transform the text into:

> a story of love and death wherein two beings tear each other apart, with moors and cliffs in the background; a quasi-mystical hymn to nature; and at its telluric depths, a poem in the manner of Giono, in which madness lurks at every twist of the rocky road. I did not feel I was betraying Maupassant: in my own way, I feel I apprehended him. Leaving aside the description of the humble people which had made him successful, I was only interested in the intoxication of the conquered flesh that, as in *Le Horla*, gradually pushed Maupassant into madness.[15]

Astruc's interpretations are clearly visible in the final version. While respecting the narrative framework of the original novel, he directed it in a strictly personal manner, playing upon the insertion of the actors' bodies into the natural space of the cliffs of Cotentin, where he shot the film in the middle of a harsh autumn. He tyrannized his actors so as to rid them of all the tics of psychologizing dramaturgy that dominated the usual acting style of 1950s literary cinema. Christian Marquand played Julien, the brutal husband of the sentimental heroine; nevertheless, Astruc never reduced him to caricature. Julian is an impassive fellow, silent and penniless, who is primarily interested in hunting. He remains blind to the effusive emotions of his young bride, and Astruc's *mise-en-scène* describes the lack of affective communication between the two characters. According to Astruc:

> Although working on a subject that was not my own, with a crew that was hostile toward me, and a star [Schell] who obeyed me only because she was forced to do so, I managed to slip in all my obsessions: my lifelong "misogyny," my rather infantile eroticism, but also my fervor for lyricism, the attraction I hold for wide open spaces, and my innate taste for grandeur and beauty. To make a long story short, despite Maria Schell, I made, as Jacques Siclier would later say, that which is most precious in the world: a *film d'auteur*.[16]

As we saw previously, critic Jean-Luc Godard was not wrong. The decoupage in *One Life* fully belonged to modern storytelling tactics, or *écriture*, and had no equivalent in 1958 French film production. One need only look at the movie's opening establishing shots, the heroine running across the dunes, the yellow dress of her maid Rosalie (Pascale Petit), for evidence. It is also obvious in the masterful high-angle long take sequence that reveals the first encounter between the future married couple on the port's seawall where the man stands on the lookout: "To show that for a man of the woods and a woman of soul to marry is madness," as Godard writes.[17]

The Front Page of the Journal *Arts*

Truffaut's arguments incited passionate debates at the heart of specialized criticism, such as in the pages of *Cahiers du Cinéma*. His series of articles published in the weekly journal *Arts*, beginning in 1956, had a very different audience, since this publication had a much wider appeal than that of the very specialized monthly on film criticism. The *Arts* readership reached its peak in the issue published for the Festival at Cannes, May 15, 1957. This special issue came equipped with a certain sense of sensationalism, promising to "severely reveal the truth about the men and methods of French cinema." The title alone was a platform in itself – "You are Witnesses in this Trial: The French Cinema is being Crushed Under the Weight of its False Legends" – and the article was splashed across all six columns of the front page.

Truffaut's points were the following:

1. The excuse invoked by the directors, that they have no control over subject-matter, is nothing but a pretext to justify their cowardice.
2. The crisis of French cinema is nothing but a crisis of courage and thus of "virility."
3. One can make an excellent film with a very low budget of roughly $10,000.
4. A director like Roberto Rossellini, "the Bernard Palissy of the cinema," proves by his production practices that risk pays.

5. The large fees offered to Brigitte Bardot are not at all scandalous; she deserves them.
6. There are too many winks and tongue-in-cheek comments in the so-called "intelligent" cinema.
7. There are no bad films, only mediocre directors.
8. Tomorrow's films will be made by adventurers.

Within these slogans there is a great deal of provocation and an undeniable panache. Many established filmmakers never forgave him for this iconoclastic discourse. Truffaut deliberately underestimated censorship and, even more, the pre-censorship of scripts, which barred all directors from mentioning the colonial wars, and especially Algeria, even though French society at the time was daily being influenced by them. We will avoid commenting upon the comparison between courage and virility and the justification of Bardot's fees as arising from polemical insolence. But we will hear more about his hostility toward large budgets which impede artistic freedom. This will be one of the fundamental creeds of the New Wave's ethics, and Truffaut is, to a certain degree, clairvoyant in pointing out that tomorrow's films would be made by adventurers.

The *Politique des Auteurs*

The argument inaugurated by Truffaut in 1954 was nothing less than the springboard for the affirmation of a principle that he would go on to define with the help of several other critics, especially Godard, Eric Rohmer, and Jacques Rivette, in the next few years. It concerns the *"politique des auteurs"* or auteur policy, which is attributed, sometimes mistakenly, to André Bazin, who was in fact quite wary of this group of "young Turks" as he and *Cahiers du Cinéma* co-editor Jacques Doniol-Valcroze quickly labeled them. Truffaut even demonstrated this policy in a critical review of a fairly commercial, impersonal film by Jacques Becker, *Ali Baba et les quarantes voleurs* (*Ali Baba and the Forty Thieves*, 1954), which was co-produced by its star, the popular Fernandel. Truffaut's points were the following:

1. There is only one auteur of a film and that is the director. All creative paternity is denied the scriptwriter, who does nothing more than supply the raw material to the auteur.
2. This policy is very selective, based on subjective judgments of value. Some directors are auteurs: Renoir, Bresson, Ophuls, etc. Others will never be considered as such, even if they manage to make a film that is praised, as was the case with Claude Autant-Lara, whose *Four Bags Full* was very well liked by Truffaut.
3. "There are no works, there are only auteurs." This aphorism from Giraudoux allowed Truffaut to propose that a failed film by an auteur, such as Becker's *Ali Baba*, would be more interesting than an apparently successful movie by a "director," as in the case of *Monsieur Ripois* by René Clément.

This *politique* was thus provocative and paradoxical by choice. It denied the collective nature of the whole cinematic creation process. It reduced scriptwriting to a secondary level. Only directing, defined as the concern of the auteur, is taken into account. For Truffaut, it also involved violently opposing those critics who, "because of their sterilizing effect of old age, even senility," were contemptuous of the later Hollywood films of Abel Gance, Fritz Lang, Alfred Hitchcock, Howard Hawks, Roberto Rossellini, and Jean Renoir. "Despite its script, pummeled by 10 or 12 people, 10 or 12 people too many, except for Becker, *Ali Baba* is a film from an auteur, an auteur who has achieved an exceptional mastery, an auteur of films."[18]

That same issue of *Cahiers* included two other very important selections: one was the publication of a long interview with Alfred Hitchcock, tape-recorded by Truffaut and Claude Chabrol, which was a new practice that had just been inaugurated at *Cahiers* with a prior interview of Jacques Becker. Second, André Bazin wrote to clarify the editors' position in relation to the excesses of those he calls the "young Turks," whom he lists as Maurice Schérer, which was the real name for Eric Rohmer, Truffaut, Jacques Rivette, Chabrol, and Robert Lachenay; the latter was occasionally used as a pseudonym by Truffaut, who thus makes it onto the list twice. In his essay, Bazin poses the question, "How can one be a 'Hitchcocko-

Hawksian?' " in part because he never shared these young critics' enthusiasm for the director of *Rebecca* (Hitchcock, 1940) and he made it perfectly clear he preferred the Hawks of *Scarface* (1932) to that of *Gentlemen Prefer Blondes* (1953): "For my part, I deplore Hollywood's ideological sterilization and its increasing timidity about treating 'grand subjects' freely."[19] Yet, Bazin also acted as an advocate for the positions taken by the young critics, defending their analytical competence, since they had seen each film they discussed five or six times; moreover, "they are vigilant about refusing to *reduce* the cinema to what it expresses only." Bazin affirms here that evaluating a film cannot be done simply by considering its scenario and themes: "But, if they prize *mise-en-scène* it is because they discern within it to a great extent the very material of film, an organization of beings and things that make up its meaning, moral as well as aesthetic. . . . Every technique refers to metaphysics."[20] This formula would prove quite successful; it was picked up by Godard, Rivette, and Luc Moullet before becoming a commonplace of current journalistic criticism. Bazin clearly pointed out here that a film must be appreciated for the formal elements it mobilizes, its "signifying material," as a 1960s semiotician would say, and not because of its thematic project, much less the intentions of its auteur.

The theme of "technique that refers to metaphysics" is developed by Godard in a round table at *Cahiers du Cinéma* devoted to *Hiroshima mon amour* (Resnais, 1959), with its famous formula "a tracking shot is a matter of morality": "There is one thing that bothers me in *Hiroshima*, and that also irritated me in *Nuit et brouillard* (*Night and Fog*, Resnais, 1955), which is a certain ease at presenting scenes of horror, because one quickly goes beyond aesthetics."[21]

Next, it was Jacques Rivette's turn to pick up and develop the same idea (which would also become the basis for the critical doctrine followed by Serge Daney at *Cahiers* 20 years later), in an article entitled "On Abjection," devoted to Gillo Pontecorvo's film *Kapo* (1960):

Look, however, at the shot where Riva commits suicide by throwing himself upon the electrified barbed wire fence; any man who decides at that moment to dolly in to reframe the body in a low-angle shot, taking care to capture precisely the hand stretched out at a diagonal for its final framing, is a person who has a right to nothing but the deepest contempt.[22]

This moral issue arose every time the cinema confronted subjects as serious as the extermination of Jews by the Nazi Holocaust, a problem that cropped up again when Steven Spielberg adapted Thomas Keneally's book *Schindler's List* (1993) with a spectacular budget that allowed him to recreate the death camp at Auschwitz inside a studio and to film it in cinemascope.

The American Model

The critical doctrine at *Cahiers du Cinéma* was also founded on the idea of relation and legacy within the history of aesthetic forms. Godard had often maintained that he belonged to a generation of directors who, for the first time, had a deep knowledge of the history of cinema and its great auteurs. This claim is a bit exaggerated since, beginning in 1916–18, the French cinema saw an anterior generation of critic-filmmakers who also defined their aesthetic program around their admiration for certain works and auteurs; for example, they praised the American and Scandinavian cinemas, including directors Thomas Ince and Victor Sjöström. Moreover, Henri Langlois employed the expression "first wave" to designate the critical school that revolved around Louis Delluc, including auteurs Germaine Dulac, Jean Epstein, and Abel Gance. All of which indicates that the New Wave was not the first. This admiration for the American cinema in particular was thus already an old tradition in French criticism, though the *Cahiers* school revived it with remarkable dynamism, in opposition to the dominant critical trends of the 1950s which privileged the serious messages of such "*grands auteurs*" as Sergei Eisenstein, Vittorio de Sica, or Carl Dreyer. Further, the *Cahiers* critics based their praise in part on the cult of the "B movie," which is to say lower budget films with no big star that were produced in great quantity during this period.

Jean-Pierre Melville was not a film critic, but his erudite passion for American detective movies was already legendary at the time, and he exercised a very strong influence on Truffaut's and Godard's discovery of the "little masters of the 'B' pictures" at the beginning of the 1950s. This cult of the "B movie" is particularly easy to spot in *Bob le flambeur* (*Bob the Gambler*), which Melville directed in 1955. The original story was written by Melville, who adapted the tale with the help of Auguste Le Breton, a dialogue writer. But Melville was also the art director and production manager for the film, which he co-produced with his own firm, Jenner Productions, and shot in the small studio space of the same name. It is the auteur's voice that introduces the film in voice-over, describing the neighborhoods of Pigalle and Montmartre in the early morning: "As told in Montmartre, here is the curious tale of . . ." then the phrase is interrupted at the moment when the written title appears (covered by a jazz theme on a trumpet), but the voice returns in a tone somewhere between documentary and irony, pointing out "this charwoman who is very late crossing paths with this young girl who is very 'advanced' for her years." Bob, a tired gangster, played with nonchalance by Roger Duchesne, appears playing poker with several acolytes in the back of a night club.

What is striking in this opening scene is the strong influence of the American model, which is perceptible in the presence of the US Navy men who pick up the girls (one of whom calls out "Come on baby, une petite promenade sur la moto?"), the exaggerated lighting, typical of film noir in the early 1950s, and Bob's gestures in his raincoat and hat. However, much like the films of Jules Dassin and Robert Wise, the detective story is strongly linked to a description of the real location, as in a documentary. Melville takes the time to describe the Place Pigalle, the ballet of the city truck spraying away the remnants of the night's garbage accompanied by an organ ritornello by Barbarie, and the meeting between the police commissioner played by Guy Decomble (who would later play the teacher in *The 400 Blows*) and Bob, the tired gambler. The latter even sees his face in a mirror at one point, says, in voice-over, "Good face for a hoodlum," before heading off to buy his morning paper at the news-stand. All of these elements will be literally recaptured by Jean-Luc Godard when he directs *Breathless* four years later. However, Godard amplifies and makes more explicit the American references by showing a photo of Humphrey Bogart, filming the offices of the *New York Herald Tribune*, and citing extracts from

Jean-Pierre Melville acts in Godard's *Breathless* (Godard, 1960).
Produced by Les Films de Georges de Beauregard

films when his characters have to hide out in the MacMahon movie theater, which shows American films exclusively, and most of all by dedicating the film to Monogram Pictures, the studio that produced the B-series movie by Joseph H. Lewis, *Gun Crazy* (1949), which Godard the critic had admired so much. Truffaut's *Shoot the Piano Player*, a very personal adaptation of the American novel by David Goodis, fits within this same tradition, playing with nostalgic citations and sudden shifts of tone.

The New Wave: An "Artistic School"

"An artistic school brings together artists with a shared tendency," according to standard dictionary entries. Let us summarize here the points we outlined earlier that help define a school:

- a body of critical doctrine for the New Wave is formed by the *politique des auteurs* as practiced by the group of "Hitchcocko-Hawksians;"
- the creative aesthetic program springing from that same group and their *politique*: to make personal films, written and conceived by their auteur;
- a group of works responding to these criteria, consisted of the first films by Chabrol, Truffaut, Kast, Doniol-Valcroze, Godard, Rivette, and Rohmer: *Le Beau Serge*, *The 400 Blows*, *Le Bel Âge*, *L'Eau à la bouche* (*A Game for Six Lovers*, 1960), *Breathless*, *Paris Belongs to Us*, and *The Sign of Leo*;
- the group of artists includes those mentioned above, but defining the limits of membership nonetheless poses problems, which we will return to shortly;
- editorial support, of course, was provided by *Cahiers du Cinéma*;
- the promotional strategy was conceived and put into practice by François Truffaut, essentially in the pages of the weekly *Arts*; this initiative made him, incontestably, the group's leader;
- as for a theoretician, that was André Bazin, whose previous articles were collected and published after his death, in 1958, in four thin volumes under the programmatic title *What is Cinema?* This series was condensed into two volumes for the English-language version;
- finally, their adversaries formed vast battalions.

The adversaries referred to in this list were, chiefly, the directors of the "Tradition of Quality" whom Truffaut had pointed out and named. They also included scriptwriters. Henri Jeanson and Michel Audiard did not miss the opportunity to fly to the aid of Jean Aurenche and Pierre Bost. Other adversaries included critics from daily and weekly newspapers and magazines, as well as from monthly film journals, including *Positif* and *Premier Plan*, all of whom were very hostile to the theories espoused by the *Cahiers* team. After the surprise triumph of the New Wave filmmakers at the 1959 Cannes Film Festival, their critics launched an extremely intense counter-offensive that would mark the whole of the next decade. One can still see the effects 20 or 30 years later in the unflattering accounts of the New Wave in Francis Courtade's *Les Malédictions du cinéma français* (*The Curses of the*

French Cinema) or Freddy Buache's *Le Cinéma français des années soixante* (*French Cinema of the 1960s*).[23]

Ever since the 1970s, at every hint of a crisis in film attendance, someone drags out the specter of the New Wave, which is always blamed for having begun the decline in film attendance. The rehabilitation of the "quality" cinema was undertaken by directors from the generations that came after the New Wave. Bertrand Tavernier, a former *Positif* critic, did not hesitate to ask Jean Aurenche and Pierre Bost to collaborate on the scripts for his films, beginning with *L'Horloger de Saint-Paul* (*The Clockmaker of Saint Paul*, 1974). The writers and directors of the *café-théatre*, organized around actor Gérard Jugnot and writer Jean-Marie Poiré, have overwhelmingly returned to the words of the author and the old divisions between scenarist / dialogue writer / director.

With the death of François Truffaut in 1984, Claude Autant-Lara persevered in his hatred even beyond his enemy's grave. Autant-Lara was certainly not alone.

Chapter Three
A Mode of Production and Distribution

An Economic Concept: "The Small Budget Film," Was it Myth or Reality?

I T HAS OFTEN BEEN ASSUMED that the New Wave provoked a sudden break in the production practices of French cinema, by favoring small budget films. In an industry characterized by an inflationary spiral of ever-increasing production costs, this phenomenon is sufficiently original to warrant investigation. Did most of the films considered to be part of this movement correspond to this notion of a small budget? We would first have to ask: what, in 1959, was a "small budget" movie?

The average cost of a film increased from roughly $218,000 in 1955 to $300,000 in 1959. That year, at the moment of the emergence of the New Wave, 133 French films were produced; of these, 33 cost more than $400,000 and 74 cost more than $200,000. That leaves 26 films with a budget of less than $200,000, or "low budget productions;" however, that can hardly be used as an adequate criterion for movies to qualify as "New Wave."[1] Even so, this budgetary trait has often been employed to establish a genealogy for the movement. It involves, primarily, "marginal" films produced outside the dominant commercial system.

Two Small Budget Films, "Outside the System"

From the point of view of their mode of production, two titles are often imposed as reference points: Jean-Pierre Melville's self-produced *Silence of the Sea*, 1947, and Agnes Varda's *La Pointe courte* (*Short Point*), made seven years later, in 1954. Both of these film projects figure largely in the "chronology of new French cinema landmarks" proposed in the December 1962 special issue of *Cahiers du Cinéma* devoted to the New Wave; that chart was an expanded version of Labarthe's genealogical list.

Jean-Pierre Melville (which was a pseudonym for Jean-Pierre Grumbach, born 1917) had proclaimed himself "inventor of the New Wave": "which is an artisanal system of production, shot in real locations, without stars, with minimal equipment and very fast film stock, without first worrying about a distributor, or official authorization, or servitude of any sort."[2] Melville had already shot under just such conditions back in 1945 when he made a short film, *24 Hours in the Life of a Clown*, though short films were often shot on tiny budgets. He was much more audacious when, in 1947, he leapt into producing and directing an adaptation of the novel *Silence of the Sea* without even getting the permission of the author, much less paying any rights, and without having received authorization to film from the Centre nationale de la cinématographie (CNC). The budget was minimal, $18,000 (though some sources put it at even less), at a time when the average cost for a French film was between $100,000 and $120,000. None of his collaborators had professional cards or belonged to the official guilds or unions, which dragged out the post-production process for a very long time, as Melville tried to work things out with the CNC after the actual filming was already finished.

A private premiere of *Silence of the Sea* took place in November 1948, but its commercial release did not occur until April 1949. The movie met with strong critical and even popular success, and thus proved a new lesson that would take ten years to really catch on: a very low budget film (meaning roughly a tenth of the average budget), could possess real aesthetic qualities and also generate good business at the box office. *Silence of the Sea* remained an isolated example, even though Melville directed and produced another feature in 1949, which was another adaptation, this time of Jean Cocteau's *Parents terribles* (*The Strange Ones*), with full agreement from the author. However, this film was a failure at the box office, requiring Melville to accept a commercial assignment to direct a movie he did not write, adapt, or produce: *Quand tu liras cette lettre* (*When You Read this Letter*, 1953).

The second example was even more atypical. When she launched into her adventure of producing *La Pointe courte*, Agnes Varda, a photographer for the National Theater in Paris, was only 26 years old. Her initial budget was targeted at $24,000, but she had to reduce it to $14,000, with herself, the crew, and actors all working as a cooperative, the Ciné Tamaris Company. They shot for several weeks on location in the fishing village of La Pointe Courte on the Mediterranean coast near Sète, where they used natural interiors and exteriors:

> Tamaris Films only managed to gather one quarter of the necessary production costs. Hence the proposal made to the actors and technicians to form a cooperative that would own 35 percent of the film. In effect, that was to say: no one gets paid during filming. It took 13 years to reimburse them their share of the work-capital. The film was only made thanks to the generosity of the actors Silvia Monfort and Philippe Noiret, and to the enthusiasm of the young crew members. Most of all, thanks went to Carlos Vilardebo, catalyst of my dream project and of my desire to tell the life of the fishermen at La Pointe Courte and their families, whom I really loved.[3]

Here again, the film was directed totally outside the industrial circuit; though shot in 35 mm, it was made without authorization because it did not follow the rules established by the CNC. It was thus considered to be the equivalent of a 16mm film: an amateur production that could not be exhibited commercially. No distributor would agree to take it on. In 1956, two years after its completion, *La Pointe courte* nonetheless received access to a Studio Parnasse movie theater, thanks to the French Association for "Art et Essai" Cinemas; it won critical praise during its two-week run. Nonetheless, the production could not recoup its funds. The production experience of *La Pointe courte* was valuable in demonstrating to future directors the crucial importance of the distributor. Yet it is important to clarify that Varda's film was not the only one in this situation: several dozen feature-length films produced within and outside the commercial circuit remained unseen during the 1950s, which is a phenomenon we will revisit when discussing the distribution of the eventual New Wave films.

The lessons on small budget filmmaking offered by these two directors is not sufficiently conclusive. Melville had to resign himself to accepting an impersonal assignment after his first failure. Agnès Varda could not even enter her film in competition for the CNC competition for production aid, since it was made outside the system, so she began making a series of short films before being able to return to feature film production eight years later, following the successes of Chabrol, Truffaut, and Godard during the years 1958–60. The myth of small budget projects earning solid profits would not really take shape until a number of consecutive titles saw large commercial successes, and even then the phenomenon would not arrive until spring of 1959 and would last just two years.

Good Economic Health

At the end of the 1950s, French cinema was in very good economic shape. The production sector had overall earnings of 1.3 billion old francs from production costs of 7.4 billion francs, according to the findings of Jacques Ploquin, based on a survey of the economic conditions of the government that was carried out in December 1956. If we look to 1952 to determine the profitability of the 123 films produced that year, we notice that their box office figures reveal that 61 films made money, while 62 lost money. Of the 61 profitable movies, the average profit margin was $85,000. For the other 62, their average losses were at $40,000 while their average costs were $110,000. The numbers reveal that it was the lower-cost films that most often lost money. Thus, it was not for reasons of financial rationalization that small budget films were considered advantageous, but rather the reasons were initially aesthetic (though of course they became economic when the films began eventually to make money).

Admittedly, it was the big budget movies that proved to be top at the box office. In 1955 the leaders were *Napoleon* (Sacha Guitry), *Les Diaboliques* (Clouzot), and *The Red and the Black* (Autant-Lara); for 1956 the top money-makers were *The Grand Maneuver* (René Clair), *The Silent World* (Malle and Cousteau), and *Si Paris nous était conté* (*If Paris had Listened to Us*, Guitry, again). All of these are historical frescoes, costume dramas, and literary adaptations. The only exception joining the list is Commander Cousteau's movie, but it represents the documentary genre, which, once every 20 years or so, manages an exceptional triumph, as *Microcosmos* (Claude Nuridsany and Marie Pérennou) did in 1996.

With the beginning of the 1957 movie season, three films imposed themselves commercially: *The Hunchback of Notre Dame* (Delannoy), *Four Bags Full* (Autant-Lara), and *Gervaise* (Clément). These were the three films attacked by the editors at *Cahiers du Cinéma* in their May 1957, round table article, "Six Characters in Search of Auteurs," while they would also go after Jacques Becker for *Ali Baba and the Forty Thieves* (1954) and *The Adventures of Arsène Lupin* (1957), despite the contradiction that Truffaut had voiced unwavering support for Becker in the name of his own theory.

In opening this historic issue of *Cahiers* devoted to the "The Situation of French Cinema," they found a first-class spokesperson in the director of the CNC, Jacques Flaud, who was interviewed by Jacques Doniol-Valcroze and André Bazin. One fact recurs in all his responses: the cinema's economic health was very good but its artistic situation was troubling. This analysis found a favorable echo in the pages of *Cahiers*. The good economic health had two causes: first, the high level of attendance, which, we can recall, was made up of 423 million tickets sold in 1947 and 411 million in 1957, with only a slight drop in 1952, making an average of 390 entries for the years 1947–57. Second, French films were largely dominating the marketplace, with American competition only really manifesting itself later in the 1960s. Jacques Flaud pointed out that during this period French cinema exported well: in 1956, nearly 40 percent of receipts came from foreign markets. But he also raised a third cause: the intervention by the state with its "Film Aid" scheme, begun in 1948 and improved in 1953. Flaud even saw this automatic aid as providing the principal source of the recent prosperity and asked whether perhaps the current artistic sclerosis might not result from "this silly security, brought on by the aid."

A Subsidized Cinema

The first law, voted into existence in September 1948, decreed a "special additional tax" levied on box office tickets to establish a "development fund," later rebaptized "support fund." It encouraged more thrift within the profession by instituting an obligatory deduction in advance on receipts which could then be recuperated to be used on another film. This method of forced auto-financing was destined to intensify national production in the face of the scarcity of capital and the threat of economic and cultural colonialization of France brought on by the affluence of American films after World War II. The special tax on receipts hit all tickets sold, including those for imported films, so domestic French production benefited from aid supported in part by foreign films. This was a typical protectionist measure, considered in 1948 to be "temporary aid funds," but continually reapplied ever since under different methods which still today help support French film production.

The new law in 1953 retained the same principles but added several new elements, the most important being the introduction of the criterion of quality. Henceforth, the *quality* of a film would warrant a reward, or at least encouragement. Films benefiting from this provision must be French and "of a nature to serve the cause of French cinema or to open new perspectives on cinematic art." However, it was necessary to await the Order in Council of May 1955 before certain films could begin to benefit from this "quality bonus."

In 1956, the director of the CNC denounced the disastrous effects of an automatic aid system that gave creative talent an industrial frame of mind and made producers think more like exporters, since the amount of aid increased with receipts. The consequence of the aid rules was to favor films dealing with relatively facile subjects, featuring international stars, shot from stories by known writers from tales that had already proven their marketability in earlier filmed versions. Hence, there were more adaptations and remakes, "films that resort to proven talents and established actors with international, commercial reputations." These arguments were the institutional versions of the more polemical and personal views of François Truffaut. Jacques Flaud just went as far as stimulating the ardor of the producers, encouraging them to take greater risks, try out new actors, and to envision an artistic renewal, heading in the direction of a cinematic rejuvenation and reawakening. This official program was announced at the beginning of 1957 and helps us understand why the CNC would look favorably upon the first productions by Claude Chabrol and François Truffaut, allowing both their small companies to shoot outside the rules with smaller crews, which greatly angered the technicians' unions.

In 1956, several films benefited immediately from this quality aid package, which totaled $220,000. They included *Mitsou* (Jacqueline Audry), *A Man Escaped* (Robert Bresson), *Grand'Rue* (*Main Street*, Juan Antonio Bardem), and *Sikkim, terre sècrete* (*Sikkim, Secret Land*, Serge Bourguignon), with Bresson's feature alone obtaining $100,000 of the total. *A Man Escaped* had been considered "unexploitable" by distributors, but the aid package enabled it to be shown, and it recouped its entire aid amount following its very unexpected commercial success. Bresson's daring producer, Jean Thuillier, was thus encouraged in his decision to take risks. We should also point out that it was Georges de Beauregard who received aid for his production of Bardem's *Main Street*, before going on to produce Jean-Luc Godard's first films.

In 1957, a number of first films received quality aid packages, including *Goha* by Jacques Baratier, *Mort en fraude* (*Fugitive in Saigon*) by Marcel Camus, Chabrol's *Le Beau Serge*, *Un amour de poche* (*Girl in his Pocket*) by Pierre Kast, and Louis Malle's *Elevator to the Gallows*. As a result, competition for aid would play a decisive role in the emergence of the New Wave the next year. This motivating factor confirms that the movement did not appear by "spontaneous generation," despite the chance inheritance by Claude Chabrol and the timely marriage of François Truffaut, all of which we will discuss further on.

The Denunciation of Blockbuster Super-Productions

There were some central figures among those debating the French cinema who were violently opposed to expensive films. The scapegoat for this position was *The Hunchback of Notre Dame*, directed by Jean Delannoy and distributed by Ignace Morgenstern, the future father-in-law of François Truffaut, who owned Paris-Films Production and Cocinor Distribution. Delannoy's movie broke all box office records for the 1956–7 season, though Morgenstern told Roger Leenhardt, "I don't pretend that this was a masterpiece, but I do modestly believe that we made an honorable imitation of the large-scale American productions that have allowed Hollywood to turn out, moreover, some extremely interesting films."[4] It was this strategy that Jacques Rivette violently denounced:

> This film exists and it is sure to bring in plenty of money; we are not going to see it, that's all. It becomes serious when talented directors are asked to make *The Hunchback of Notre Dame*. And, what is even more serious is the moment when these talented directors start to accept making films like these while having an ulterior motive in mind. They too will shoot an $800,000 movie because that allows them to be considered a big French director because they will make a great deal of money, but at the same time they plan to tuck personal little alibis or clever bits in, but this will not make it a better film, nor will it make it into a *film d'auteur*.[5]

The directors specifically targeted by Rivette here included Claude Autant-Lara and Henri-Georges Clouzot, but also René Clément, whose last film *Gervaise* had been singled out by André Bazin as vacuous. The "characters in search of auteurs" at this round table expressed their disappointment in regard to the recent evolution of the movies by Clouzot, Clément, and Jacques Becker: "In spite of their great successes . . . [they] failed because they thought that finding a style was all it took to create a new soul for French cinema."[6] *The Adventures of Arsène Lupin* and *Gervaise* were then summarized by Bazin as "the most accomplished films by Becker and Clément, but also their most empty." This result was attributed to the conditions of production.

Rivette repeated Truffaut's slogan, proclaimed in his *Arts* editorial: Clouzot, Clément, and Autant-Lara were three big directors found guilty because they were afraid to take risks and they were corrupted by money. He then outlined his provocative aphorism: "What is most lacking in French cinema is a spirit of poverty. Its only hope now lies in . . . new directors taking those risks making films with $40,000 or $60,000, perhaps even less, and filming with whatever turns up."[7] This is precisely what Rivette himself would do the following year, when he threw himself into the adventure of making *Paris Belongs to Us*, whose chaotic direction would drag out for months, with many interruptions due to financial problems, and which could only start up again each time thanks to support from Chabrol and Truffaut.

This strong aversion toward big budgets remained a constant concern of the New Wave. When, a few years later, Godard agreed to compromise by hiring the most expensive star for an international co-production with producers Joe Levine and Carlo Ponti, he repeatedly stated that, discounting the salary paid to the main actress, his was a low budget film. The main actress in question was, of course, Brigitte Bardot, who was paid $500,000 out of the $1,000,000 total budget for *Contempt*. And François Truffaut would later strive to follow larger budget films featuring one or two stars with a low budget film, as he did with *L'Enfant sauvage* (*Wild Child*), which was made right after *La Sirène du Mississippi* (*Mississippi Mermaid*) in 1969.

Self-Produced Films

To carry out this new practice of "at risk" production, new producers were needed. Several first films have come to be considered as trailblazers, announcing the phenomenon that would then spread during the spring of 1959. We have already cited the earlier cases of Melville's and Varda's first features, which were produced too far beyond the norms to be considered part of any school.

Among other precursors, *Les Dernières Vacances* (*The Last Vacation*, 1947), produced by Pierre Gérin and directed by Roger Leenhardt, and Astruc's *Bad Encounters*, were two films by critic-theorists and collaborators at *Cahiers du Cinéma*. However, both were produced under rather conventional processes in operation during that era. Astruc's second feature, *One Life*, was a literary adaptation featuring an international star, Maria Schell, and co-produced by Annie Dorfmann, producer of the recent big budget hit *Gervaise*. Thus, even Astruc's first features failed to use the conditions of production that would define the New Wave.

Louis Malle, by contrast, made his debut with a very atypical project, *The Silent World*, which became one of the big money-makers of 1956. But he was really just the young technical consultant; it was clearly a film by commander Jacques Cousteau who already displayed a very media-savvy talent. Malle's next feature, made in a much more personal environment, was a conventional production based on a mediocre detective novel by Noel Calef, *Elevator to the Gallows* (1957), which was adapted with the help of Roger Nimier. The most original aspect of this movie was its soundtrack, composed by Miles Davis. Yet, unlike many later New Wave directors, Malle had never worked as a critic, but had studied at the French film school IDHEC before working briefly as an assistant director to Robert Bresson on his *A Man Escaped*. Malle's intinerary toward feature filmmaking was therefore very traditional.

Finally, *And God Created Woman*, directed by Roger Vadim in 1956, displayed a novelty that strongly impressed Truffaut and Godard, but it too was a classic production by Raoul Lévy, built around an international star, Curt Jurgens, who had just come from a huge success in *Michel Strogoff*, itself an international co-production directed by Carmine Gallone.

It was Claude Chabrol who, by producing his own *Le Beau Serge*, thanks to a family inheritance, showed the way. Previously, Eric Rohmer, Jacques Rivette, Pierre Kast, Truffaut, and Godard had only managed to make short films, a number of which had been awarded quality aid grants reserved for films in short format. Nevertheless, a cooperative production project had been hatched during 1958, involving several critics at *Cahiers du Cinéma* and several more experienced directors like Alain Resnais. According to Chabrol:

> To make films, we came up with a sort of cooperative. It was understood that Resnais, who was one of our friends and whose short films we had praised, would direct his first feature with Rivette as his assistant director. Next, Rivette would direct his own first film with Truffaut as assistant. Truffaut would take his turn, assisted by Charles Bitsch. When Bitsch got his turn to direct, I would be his assistant, etc. This conveyor belt system was not without merit, but it never did get under way.[8]

Claude Chabrol was the son of a pharmacist, originally from the Creuse region in south-central France, who began writing for *Cahiers* in 1953. He also wrote several detective stories for *Mystère* magazine and worked as a publicity assistant for Twentieth-Century Fox in Paris. In June, 1952 he had married in Marseilles; later, he and his wife inherited $64,000 from her grandmother. He invested the money in creating his own film production company, AJYM Films, named for his wife Agnès, and sons Jean-Yves and Mathieu. In 1956, in an alliance with producer Pierre Braunberger, Chabrol produced AJYM's first short film, directed by his friend Jacques Rivette, entitled *Coup du berger*. Jacques Doniol-Valcroze and Jean-Claude Brialy were the featured actors. This short film, shot in 35 mm, could be considered the first professional production accomplished by the New Wave, since the previous shorts by Truffaut, Rohmer, and Godard had all been filmed in 16 mm, a format which, at the time, was considered "non-professional."

Next, Chabrol decided to leap into feature filmmaking. He wrote two scripts, *Le Beau Serge* and *The Cousins*, selecting to produce the former first because it would be cheaper. The CNC provided him with a temporary authorization to film and the production took place over nine weeks, from December 1957 until February 1958. It was filmed on location in Sardent, a small village in Creuse where Chabrol, as a child, had spent four years during the Occupation. The script was partially autobiographical: Brialy plays the part of a Parisian, François, a verbal stand-in for Chabrol. The two shared many personality traits. The character of Serge, played by Gérard Blain, was partially inspired by Chabrol's friend and script-assistant, Paul Gégauff.

The initial budget for *Le Beau Serge* was $76,000, but because of cost overruns brought on by the first-time director's mistakes, the final cost reached $84,000. This is still a very low budget, but, as Chabrol admitted, "it is still quite a bit for a movie with no distributor." However, he also received a *prime à la qualité* – a quality aid grant – from the CNC for $70,000, which covered the bulk of his costs. Next, the Cannes Film Festival's selection committee chose *Le Beau Serge*, but then changed its mind, accepting François Villiers' *L'Eau vive* (*The Girl and the River*, 1957) instead. Chabrol's film was nonetheless shown in Cannes, out of competition, and a production agent, Bon Amon, sold it to foreign distributors. These advance sales, together with the grant, paid off all the costs of *Le Beau Serge* before it was ever actually distributed. Chabrol could thus throw himself into his second feature, *The Cousins*, employing much of the same crew and the same lead actors, Brialy and Blain. However, a large part of this project was shot in the small sound stage at Boulogne-Billancourt studio rather than on location in natural light. The sum recuperated by Chabrol from the grant and the initial sales of *Le Beau Serge* totaled $130,000, which he then reinvested. Bob Amon even negotiated additional production funding of $50,000 from Edmond Tenoudji in a contract that guaranteed the exhibition of both Chabrol's features. Both films proved very successful in their premieres, distributed by Marceau-Cocinor, which Tenoudji had just bought from Truffaut's father-in-law, Ignace Morgenstern. *Le Beau Serge* premiered on February 11, 1959 at the Publicis cinema and at the Avenue, for a combined Parisian first run of 13 weeks, with 67,176 tickets sold. *The Cousins* did much better: premiering on March 11, 1959 at the huge Colisée and Marivaux, it ran for a total of 14 weeks, selling 258,548 tickets in Paris alone. This commercial triumph transformed the director as well as his two young lead actors, Brialy and Blain, into New Wave stars.

Simultaneously, veteran director Jean Delannoy released *Guinguette* (1959), based on a script by Henri Jeanson, and distributed for its first run to four big theaters on March 4, 1959. It featured three top French stars: Zizi Jeanmaire, Paul Meurisse, and Jean-Claude Pascal. But the film only attracted 81,802 viewers. These figures speak for themselves, and would serve as a lesson to producers and distributors over the next two seasons.

François Truffaut's entry into the profession as young director was almost equivalent to Chabrol's experience. When he began shooting his first short film in 1957, Truffaut was well known for his film articles from *Cahiers* as well as the weekly journal *Arts*. Previously, he had also been an assistant to Roberto Rossellini during 1955 and 1956, preparing and discussing a number of projects that never came about. Truffaut also wrote up a number of ideas and scripts that he tried to get produced, after having directed a short 16 mm movie, under amateurish conditions, which remained unfinished, entitled *Une visite* (*A Visit*, 1954). Then, at the Venice Film Festival in September 1956, Truffaut met his future wife, Madeleine Morgenstern, daughter of Ignace Morgenstern, president of Cocinor, one of the largest film distribution networks in France.

Thanks to help from Ignace Morgenstern, and especially his right-hand man, Marcel Berbert, Truffaut established a tiny production company of his own, Films du Carrosse, backed by a $4,000 credit line. This amount corresponds perfectly to the budget he would use for his short film, *Les Mistons* (*The Mischief Makers*), which he adapted from Maurice Pons' short story. *Les Mistons* won the young Truffaut the best director of short films award at the Brussels International Film Festival in February 1958, and was premiered in Paris at the famous Pagode theater, along with medium-length films by Jean Rouch and Colin Low.

Truffaut began preparing his next project right away, planning to make *Temps chaud* (*Hot Weather*), an adaptation of a novel by Jacques Cousseau, with producer Pierre Braunberger, but the project was delayed several times. During the spring of 1958, the anxious Truffaut persuaded Ignace Morgenstern, who had since become his father-in-law, to allow him to make a much more personal story, *The 400 Blows*, whose cost was estimated at nearly $80,000. Filming began on November 10, 1958, the day André Bazin died, and was completed on January 5, 1959. Most of the filming was accomplished in natural locations in Paris. Following its private press screening, the movie was proposed to the jury for the Cannes Film Festival, which selected it to represent France. In the meantime, the new Fifth Republic was born and, with it, a new Ministry of Cultural Affairs, directed by novelist and filmmaker André Malraux.

The 400 Blows won the Cannes prize for best director, but Marcel Berbert's real coup came with his advance sales to foreign markets: the Americans alone bid $50,000, which covered the actual $47,000 production costs. But Berbert also sold the feature to Japanese, Italian, Swiss, and Belgian distributors for a sum equivalent to double the film's costs. Thus Truffaut's film immediately made up its production costs several times over. Further, *The 400 Blows* premiered in Paris on June 3, 1959, playing in two large theaters on the Champs-Elysées – the Colisée and the Marivaux – and running for 14 weeks, attracting 261,145 spectators in Paris and, eventually, 450,000 for its French first run. Truffaut's first feature became something of a social phenomenon, seized upon by national magazines and the popular press in articles that confronted problems of unhappy childhoods and educational reforms for adolescents.

Three Producers

Though the cases of Chabrol and Truffaut were decisive in jump-starting the movement, and its repercussions in the media, thanks both to their commercial and public triumphs, they nonetheless remained exceptions. This movement of renewal in film production would also be carried out thanks to three producers who knew how to seize the historical moment: Pierre Braunberger, Anatole Dauman, and Georges de Beauregard, whose production catalogues contain several dozen of the most important French films of the 1960s.

Pierre Braunberger (born 1905), is the old veteran of the three, making his debut in 1926, producing Alberto Cavalcanti's famous *Rien que les heures* (*Nothing but Time*) and Jean Renoir's *Charleston*. His rich catalogue includes avant-garde films as well as some very commercial works, such as *Vous n'avez rien à déclarer?* (*Confessions of a Newlywed*, 1936) by Léo Joannon, starring Raimu, Marcel Aboulker's *Les Aventures des pieds nickelés* (*Adventures of Nickel-plated Feet*, 1948), or Marc Allégret's *Julietta* (1953), starring Dany Robin and Jean Marais. But Braunberger, always on the lookout for new talents, also supported Jean-Pierre Melville's *Silence of the Sea* during 1947 and 1948. He would also distribute and co-produce ethnographic films by Jean Rouch, grouped under the title *Les Fils de l'eau* (*The Water's Sons*, 1951–5), and produce François Reichenbach's documentary, *L'Amérique insolite* (*Unusual America*, 1958), which was shot with a fast new film stock and went on to be quite successful.

Braunberger would also play a decisive role in the realm of short film production by encouraging short narratives, despite that fact that most short films during this epoch were documentaries and industrial assignments. He recalled the 1930s when many first-rate shorts were produced. During 1947 and 1948 he produced shorts about famous painters and their works, including *Van Gogh*, *Guernica*, and *Gauguin* by Alain Resnais and *Toulouse-Lautrec* and *Chagall* directed by Robert Hessens. But in 1956 he decided to co-produce Jacques Rivette's *Le Coup du berger* along with Claude Chabrol. It was shot in 35 mm in Chabrol's apartment, based on a script by Rivette,

Chabrol, and Charles Bitsch, who also served as camera operator. He also backed Agnès Varda's *O Saisons, O chateaux* (*Of Seasons and Chateaux*, 1956), followed by *Les Surmenés* (*The Overworked*) by Jacques Doniol-Valcroze, *Tous les garçons s'appellent Patrick* (*All the Boys are Called Patrick*) by Godard, based on a script by Eric Rohmer, their *Charlotte et son Jules* (*Charlotte and her Jules*), and Truffaut and Godard's *Histoire d'eau* (*A Story of Water*). Thus, Braunberger is a producer who helped pave the way for the movement's appearance via his catalogue of short films. Yet, as we have emphasized, from the point of view of producers and even more the public, the realm of feature fiction films remains decisive since it is much more important in terms of institutional "visibility" and any hopes of financial returns.

During 1958 and 1959, Braunberger produced three key feature-length films, one after the other, during the New Wave's initial phase: *Me, a Black Man* and *La Pyramide humaine* (*The Human Pyramid*) by Jean Rouch, and *A Game for Six Lovers* by Jacques Doniol-Valcroze. He also continued with other Rouch films, *La Punition* (1962), *The Lion Hunt* (1965), and *Jaguar* (1967). At the beginning of the 1960s, he produced Truffaut's second feature, *Shoot the Piano Player*, Doniol-Valcroze's third, *La Dénonciation* (*The Denunciation*, 1961), and Godard's fourth, *My Life to Live*. All these movies had fairly modest budgets.

Anatole Dauman (born in Warsaw in 1925) emigrated to France and, along with Philippe Lifchitz, formed Argos Films in 1951, a niche company to make films on art, based on the model provided by the Italian documentaries of Luciano Emmer, and often produced on order for Foreign Ministers. In this manner, Dauman produced the first films by Pierre Kast, Jean Aurel, and Chris Marker. In 1953, thanks to an advance by distributor Jean Thuillier of UGC, he produced Alexandre Astruc's medium-length *Crimson Curtain*, which also received a *prime à la qualité*. Next there were Alain Resnais' *Night and Fog* and Chris Marker's *Sunday in Peking* and *Letter From Siberia*. In 1959, Argos also initiated *Hiroshima mon amour*. Further, they produced *Last Year at Marienbad* and *Chronique d'un été* (*Chronicle of a Summer*), the *cinéma vérité* manifesto by Rouch and sociologist Edgar Morin.

The Paris release of *Chronicle of a Summer* was accompanied by an article entitled "For a New Direct Cinema," written by Morin, that appeared in a January 1960 *France-Observateur* magazine:

> This film is an investigation. The milieu of research is Paris. It is not a fiction film. Its research involves real life. It is not a documentary. This investigation does not want to describe; rather, it is an experience lived by its authors and actors. It is not, strictly speaking, a sociological film. Sociological cinema investigates society. It is an ethnographic film in its purest sense: it investigates people. It involves a cinematic interrogation: "How do you live?" This entails not simply how you live (housing, work, leisure activities), but also your style of living, your attitude toward yourself and others, the way you perceive the deepest problems and how you see the solution to those problems.[9]

During the 1960s, Anatole Dauman produced veteran Roger Leenhardt's second feature film, *Le Rendez-vous de minuit* (*Rendezvous at Midnight*, 1961), co-produced Alain Resnais' third feature, *Muriel* (1963), two features by Godard, *Masculine-Feminine* (1966) and *Deux ou trois choses que je sais d'elle* (*Two or Three Things I Know About Her*, 1967), as well as two films by Robert Bresson, *Au hasard Balthazar* (1966) and *Mouchette* (1967). The budget for these 1960s films were considerably higher than the costs of comparable films by Braunberger and Georges de Beauregard. While they all became major works of the modern French cinema, they did not fit the mode of production specific to New Wave projects, since they were expensive and relied heavily upon studios and post-synchronization.

Finally, Georges de Beauregard (born in Marseille in 1920) would become Godard's producer from *Breathless* on. However, de Beauregard's career was very atypical. He began in Spain during the 1950s as an exporter of French films. In Madrid, he produced the first two features by Juan Antonio Bardem, *Death of a Cyclist* and *Main Street*, both in 1956, with the latter earning a *prime à la qualité*. Then de Beauregard came to France, where he entered into a partnership with novelist Joseph Kessel, becoming involved in a very adventurous project shot in Afghanistan, *La Passe du diable* (*Devil's Pass*), directed by Jacques Dupont and Pierre Schoendoerffer, with Raoul Coutard as cinematographer. Although *Devil's Pass* was shown at the Berlin Film Festival in 1958, it was not released until October 1959. De Beauregard fell back to making much more conventional adaptations of novels by Pierre Loti, including *Ramuntcho* and *Pêcheurs d'Islande* (*Iceland Fishermen*), both released in 1959 and directed by Schoendoerffer. They were classical productions, shot in color and the widescreen Dyaliscope process, far beyond the aesthetics of the New Wave.

Then, Jean-Luc Godard convinced de Beauregard to accept a detective script idea that he had been offered by Truffaut, and on which both had worked previously over a period of several years, based on a real anecdote in the news. De Beauregard agreed to finance the project, offering a very low budget of $80,000, the bulk of which went to actress Jean Seberg and her contractural company, Fox. The company owned by Leon Beytout and Roger Pignières, SNC, gave a much needed advance for the film's eventual distribution. Godard lived within the constraints of his contract by shooting very rapidly, in only four weeks, beginning on August 17 and finishing on September 15, 1959. The editing and post-synchronization were much more laborious, and *Breathless* was not distributed until March 16, 1960, when it premiered in four first-run theaters in Paris, running for seven weeks. It was accompanied by an incredibly dynamic promotional campaign, spearheaded by the journal *Arts*.

Breathless became a new triumph for the New Wave: 259,046 tickets were sold in Paris, followed by another 121,874 in the major towns in the rest of France. Godard's success saved de Beauregard's film company from what were becoming difficult times; Beauregard was so appreciative that he went on to produce six more Godard features, despite the fact that the second, *Le Petit Soldat*, was banned in 1960 and only released in France in 1963. His company also produced *A Woman is a Woman* (1961), *Les Carabiniers* (1963), *Contempt* (1963), *Made in USA* (1966), and, nearly ten years later, *Numéro deux* (*Number Two*, 1975).

Thus, with Godard acting as intermediary, Georges de Beauregard became the principal producer of the New Wave, producing films for Jacques Demy (*Lola*), Jacques Rozier (*Adieu Philippine*), Claude Chabrol (*The Third Lover; Landru; Marie-Chantal contre le docteur Kah*, 1965), Jean-Pierre Melville (*Leon Morin, Priest*, 1965; *Le Doulos*, 1965), Agnès Varda (*Cléo from 5 to 7*, 1962), Pierre Schoendoerffer again (*The 317th Platoon*, 1965; *Objective: 500 Million*, 1966), Jacques Rivette (*La Religieuse*,

Table 3.1 Attendance figures for older and newer generation directors

Older Generation*	Tickets sold in first run
Best results	
1. *The Cheats* (Carné, 1958)	556,203
2. *The Truth* (Clouzot, 1960)	527,026
3. *Hunchback of Notre Dame* (Delannoy, 1956)	495,071
4. *The Baron* (Delannoy, 1960)	366,168
5. *La Traversée de Paris / Four Bags Full* (Autant-Lara, 1956)	363,033
6. *Gervaise* (Clément, 1956)	357,393
7. *The Green Mare* (Autant-Lara, 1959)	320,887
Worst results	
1. *Thou Shalt Not Kill* (Autant-Lara, 1963)	21,343
2. *The Trial of Joan of Arc* (Bresson, 1963)	24,105
3. *The Mystery of Picasso* (Clouzot, 1956)	37,062
4. *La Grande Vie* (Duvivier, 1960)	43,286
5. *Boulevard* (Duvivier, 1960)	47,293
6. *When a Woman Meddles* (Allégret, 1957)	47,654
7. *Pickpocket* (Bresson, 1959)	48,612

Newer generation*	
Best results	
1. *Dangerous Liaisons* (Vadim, 1960)	693,955
2. *Love on a Pillow / The Warrior's Rest* (Vadim, 1962)	481,869
3. *The Lovers* (Malle, 1958)	451,473
4. *The Silent World* (Cousteau and Malle, 1956)	280,411
5. *The 400 Blows* (Truffaut, 1959)	261,145
6. *Breathless* (Godard, 1960)	259,046
7. *The Cousins* (Chabrol, 1959)	258,548
Worst results	
1. *Les Carabiniers* (Godard, 1963)	2,800
2. *Ophélia* (Chabrol, 1962)	6,983

Table 3.1 *Continued*

Older Generation*	Tickets sold in first run
3. *The Third Lover* (Chabrol, 1962)	8,023
4. *Les Godelureaux* (Chabrol, 1961)	23,408
5. *Portuguese Vacation* (Kast, 1963)	27,913
6. *Lola* (Demy, 1961)	43,385
7. *The Snobs* (Mocky, 1962)	44,491

* We use these labels guardedly since, aesthetically, it could be argued that Robert Bresson and Jacques Becker fit closer to the "newer generation" and Philippe de Broca and Roger Vadim are closer to the "older generation," but we have divided the directors according to the biographical lists regularly published in the New Wave era, and retained as well by historian Pierre Billard.

1966; *L'Amour fou*, 1968), and Eric Rohmer (*La Collectionneuse*, 1967). The result is an incredibly impressive filmography.

In Braunberger, Dauman, and de Beauregard, the CNC's Jacques Flaud had found three daring producers who lived up to his 1957 call for new production concepts. All that remains is for us to look at the results of the financial fates of the New Wave films compared to those of the so-called "tradition of quality."

Films by "Old and New" Directors in the Public Arena

A young American film student, Ignazio Scaglione, in an unpublished study, selected ten "older generation" directors and ten new, young directors and then compared the global attendance numbers for all their films released between 1956 and 1963. His attendance figures for the older generation – Allégret, Autant-Lara, Becker, Bresson, Carné, Christian-Jacque, Clément, Clouzot, Delannoy, and Duvivier – came to a total of 9,888,538 tickets sold in their first runs, for an average of 159,444 entries per film. For the newer generation he selected de Broca, Chabrol, Demy, Godard, Kast, Malle, Mocky, Resnais, Truffaut, and Varda. Their totals were 7,168,078, with an average of 143,361 tickets sold per film (see table 3.1). The box office results obtained by the newer directors were thus somewhat lower than those for the directors from the previous generation, but the difference is not that marked, especially given that some of the New Wave titles, such as Chabrol's *L'Oeil du malin* and *Ophélia*, or Godard's *Les Carabiniers*, had been resounding financial flops, while other films on the list, especially *Hiroshima mon amour* and *Last Year at Marienbad* by Alain Resnais, were aimed at an intellectual niche audience. Table 3.1 illustrates the contrast between the greatest financial successes and failures in each category.

Those hostile to the New Wave have always claimed that it led to the production of dozens of movies that were "unprojectable" and thus no distributor would agree to try to find them a public. Further, they then point to the New Wave's low budgets. This phenomenon of a lack of a commercial distribution contract, even on surprisingly low cost films, occurs fairly often and in all eras of film production. Typically, the problem is that the films' production is never finished because of a lack of adequate completion financing, or occasionally because of disagreements between directors and producers. However, in 1962, there were just as many New Wave films as there were "old guard" films that remained on their producers' shelves. Luc Moullet provides the list:

> In fact, there are 22 films older than 20 months (the time after which movies are considered unmarketable) and thus unreleased in Paris: *Un jour comme les autres* (*A Day Like the Others*, Bordry), *Merci Natercia* (Kast), *La Ligne de mire* (*Line of Fire*, Pollet), *L'Engrenage* (*Caught in the Gears*, Kalifa), *Sikkim* (Bourguignon), *La Mort n'est pas à vendre* (*Death is Not for Sale*, Desrumeaux), *Au coeur de la ville* (*Center of Town*, Gautherin), *Les Petits Chats* (*Kittens*, Villa), and three banned by the censor: *Morambong* (Bonnardot), *Le Petit Soldat* (Godard), *Playboys* (Felix).[10]

These 11 were all by young directors. Moullet then adds 11 titles by directors representing the older generation, some of whom have very long filmographies: *Les Copains du dimanche* (*Sunday Buddies*, Aisner, it features Jean-Paul Belmondo just before he made *Breathless*), *Ça aussi, c'est Paris* (*That too is Paris*, Cloche), *Trois Pin-ups comme ça* (*Three Pin Up Girls Please*, Bibal), *L'Or de Samory* (*Samory's Gold*, Alden), *La Blonde des tropiques* (*The Tropical Blonde*, Roy), *Un homme à vendre* (*One Man for Sale*, Labro), *Le Train de 8h 47* (*The 8:47 Train*, Pinoteau, unfinished), *Le Tout pour le tout* (*All for All*, Dally), *L'Eespionne sera à Nouméa* (*The Spy Will be at Noumea*, Péclet), *Chasse à l'homme* (*Man Hunt*, Mérenda), and *Qu'as tu fait de ta jeunesse?* (*How Did You Lose Your Youth?* Daniel). None of these films was banned by the censor, and most of them were never shown commercially.

Chapter Four
A Technical Practice, an Aesthetic

The New Wave's Aesthetic

THE NEW WAVE IS BASED ON a different manner of producing films, as we saw in the previous chapter, that privileges small budgets so as to safeguard the creative freedom of the auteur director. However, it also overturned many conventions that governed the technical practices for filmmaking in that era, from conception right up to its editing and final mix. The New Wave thereby brought a new generation of technicians, creative collaborators, camera operators, and writers into a profession that had been very closed and isolated. The New Wave aesthetic is founded on a series of choices made from the script through to the final print. In principle, it assumes, therefore, the following agenda:

1. The auteur director is also the scenarist for the film.
2. The director does not follow a strict, pre-established shooting script, leaving instead much of the filming to improvisation in the conception of sequences, dialogue, and acting.
3. The director privileges shooting in natural locations and avoids building artificial sets in the studio.
4. The director uses a small crew of only a few people.
5. The director opts for "direct sound" recorded during filming rather than relying too much on post-synchronization.

6. The director avoids depending upon overly heavy additional lighting units, and thus selects, along with the cinematographer, a very fast film stock that requires less light.
7. The director employs non-professionals as actors.
8. If the director has access to professionals, newer actors will be chosen and directed in a freer manner than conventional productions allow.

All of these choices provide for a greater sense of flexibility in the direction and endeavor to streamline as much as possible the heavy constraints typical of the commercial, industrialized cinema model. They are aimed at erasing the borders between professional and amateur cinema, and those between fiction, and documentary, or investigative films.

Films that take these strategies to their logical conclusions are very rare, but they provide the underpinnings for the creative cinematic process wrought by the New Wave. The initial model is embodied in the films of Jean Rouch, beginning in particular with *Me, a Black Man*. It would be Rouch who was the most faithful to this approach throughout the 1960s, with films like *The Human Pyramid* (1958) and *Lion Hunt* (1965). It culminated with his medium-length project, *The Punishment*, which attracted few people in its initial exhibition, but had a strong influence upon the films of Eric Rohmer during the 1970s and '80s. But these ideals are also at the heart of one of the strongest works of 1960s French cinema: *Gare du Nord*, the short film directed by Rouch for the collective manifesto *Paris vu par . . . (Six in Paris)* in 1964.

This erasure of the boundary between fiction and documentary is one of the aesthetic poles of the New Wave, influencing Rohmer, Jacques Rivette, Jacques Rozier, Jean Eustache, and Godard in some instances, and, to a certain extent during the post-New Wave period, Maurice Pialat, Philippe Garrel, and Jacques Doillon.

The other pole is dominated more by narrative. It includes auteurs with a much more novelistic conception of creation, such as Claude Chabrol, François Truffaut, Agnès Varda, Jacques Demy, Pierre Kast, and Jacques Doniol-Valcroze. To varying degrees, each of these auteur directors displays more classical cinematic practice, based on a script and pre-established dialogue, and employing post-synchronization. If they belong equally to the

New Wave movement, it is due to their low budgets, their autobiographical inspiration, and their themes tied to contemporary society and embedded in the current climate: the myth of youth, new morality, the autobiographical dimension of cinema, loose narrative, and use of digressions, among other traits.

Such was not the case for directors as important as Alain Resnais or Jean-Pierre Melville, who became associated with the New Wave during at least one stage of their career. Resnais is without a doubt a great modern filmmaker, and just as important as Jean-Luc Godard in the history of filmic forms. But his conception of a script and decoupage, his continual reliance on auteur scriptwriters, such as Marguerite Duras, Alain Robbe-Grillet, Jorge Semrun, and Jacques Sternberg, his use of studios, his direction of actors, and his notion of the soundtrack based on post-synchronization, all distance him from the New Wave aesthetic, in contrast to Jacques Rozier's *Adieu Philippine*, which burst on the scene with such intensity in 1963.

As for Jean-Pierre Melville, even if his *Silence of the Sea* foreshadowed and inspired the mode of production adopted by Chabrol and Truffaut, and even if he was able to influence the Godard of *Breathless* and the Truffaut of *Shoot the Piano Player* with his small-budget, detective film *Bob le flambeur*, which retained a very personal style, he rapidly adopted a much more classical narrative style with *Le Doulos* and *L'Aîné des Ferchaux* (*Magnet of Doom*, 1963). With these latter films and the rest of his career, Melville followed the model of American cinema in the 1930s and '40s, while trying to go beyond those conventions with an "oriental" abstraction, often labeled "mannerist," and far from the New Wave aesthetic practiced by Jean Rouch, or the Godard of *My Life to Live* and *Pierrot le fou*.

The Auteur Director

Must the director serve as his own scriptwriter? What is the actual role of improvisation in the New Wave cinema?

One of the dogmas of the *politique des auteurs*, set as a base requirement by Alexandre Astruc in 1948, was that "the scriptwriter directs his own scripts; or rather, that the scriptwriter ceases to exist, for in this kind of film-making the distinction between author and director loses all meaning."[1] This thesis remains today Astruc's most popularized point. It has become a dominant idea, structuring to a certain degree the means of access to the profession and shaping the conception of first films. Hence, the cyclical return to polemics and the dialectical affirmation, in reaction, of the importance of the scriptwriter.

But what really was the role of the scriptwriter during the New Wave? Did scriptwriters all disappear to make way for the auteur director? A close review of the subjects from New Wave films reveals that instances of the filmmaker directing scripts he or she had written were far from the norm. Very rapidly, the young auteurs regularly collaborated with new scriptwriters, and those writers only rarely went on to become new directors. We need only examine several of the key early films as reference points.

Le Beau Serge is the only film that corresponds precisely to the label "script written by the director," since Claude Chabrol wrote the film, basing it to a large extent upon his own life, especially his childhood spent in the town of Sardent during the Occupation. However, beginning with *The Cousins*, Chabrol collaborated closely with his friend Paul Gégauff, who was initially credited with the dialogue for this film, but who went on to become Chabrol's steady scriptwriter for the next decade. For *À double tour* (*Leda*, 1959), it was Gégauff who adapted Stanley Ellin's detective novel, *The Key to Nicholas Street*, for the screen. With *Les Bonnes Femmes* (*The Good Girls*, 1960), Gégauff's role was dominant in the conception of the film, its characters, and the dialogue, and the scenario was signed "Paul Gégauff, from an idea by Claude Chabrol." Though the script for *L'Oeil du malin* was written by Chabrol, that for *Ophélia* was again by Gégauff, and for *Landru* Chabrol adapted a script by Françoise Sagan.

The 400 Blows is obviously a very autobiographical film. Nonetheless, François Truffaut sought out a professional scriptwriter working in television, Marcel Moussy, for a collaboration. Moussy ended up helping to structure the script and contributed to editing the dialogue, much as Pierre Bost had done with Autant-Lara. *Shoot the Piano Player* was an adaptation of a novel by American writer David Goodis, which Truffaut then reworked with the help of Marcel Moussy. For *Jules and Jim*, Truffaut adapted Henri-Pierre Roché's novel with the help of Jean Gruault. He would again collaborate with Gruault on *Wild Child, Deux Anglaises sur le continent (Two English Girls,* 1971), and *La Chambre verte (The Green Room,* 1978).

Throughout his career, with 21 feature films, Truffaut collaborated very regularly with a core of four or five scriptwriters, with each of whom he made two or three movies: Jean-Louis Richard worked on *La Peau douce (The Soft Skin,* 1964), *Fahrenheit 451* (1966), *La Mariée était en noir (The Bride Wore Black,* 1967); Claude de Givray and Bernard Revon helped write *Baisers volés (Stolen Kisses,* 1968) and *Domicile conjugal (Bed and Board,* 1970); and Suzanne Schiffman worked on *La Nuit américaine (Day for Night,* 1973), *L'Argent de poche (Small Change,* 1976), *Le Dernier métro (The Last Metro,* 1980), *La Femme d'à côté (The Woman Next Door,* 1981), and *Vivement Dimanche (Confidentially Yours,* 1983).[2]

Breathless began from a short script written by Truffaut in 1956 and signed over to Godard for the small amount of $2,000, in June 1959. Previously, Truffaut had considered shooting it himself with Jean-Claude Brialy or Gérard Blain in the role of Poiccard, then he offered it to Edouard Molinaro who was to have made it as his first feature, instead of *Dos au mur (Back to the Wall,* 1958).[3] However, for his second feature, *Le Petit soldat,* Godard wrote the script himself.

For his third feature, *A Woman is a Woman,* Godard wrote the script based on an idea from Geneviève Cluny (which he subsequently published under his name in *Cahiers du Cinéma,* number 98, in August 1959). This story had already been filmed by Philippe de Broca under the title *Les Jeux de l'amour (Games of Love,* 1959), starring Jean-Pierre Cassel, Geneviève Cluny, and Jean-Louis Maury. However, Godard made it his own, reworking the script from the ground up, as he filmed *A Woman is a Woman* in a very personal manner. Similarly, very little remains of the play by Benjamin Joppolo in Godard's *Les Carabiniers,* though the titles list Jean Gruault and even Roberto Rossellini as aiding in the adaptation. And for *Pierrot le fou* and *Band of Outsiders,* almost nothing remains of the source detective novels. They were only used to reassure the co-producers during the early stages of the productions.

Thus, it is Godard who pushes furthest this idea of a director becoming auteur of his own narrative material, since, with him, the classical notion of a script gradually loses any meaning, especially by the point of *Made in USA* (1966) and *Symphony for the Devil/ One Plus One* (1968). Godard explicitly acknowledges the economic constraints of the script-as-merchandise during his highly ironic prologue to *Tout va bien*, in 1972, when a character explains, "To make a film you need stars and a story."

The original script for Eric Rohmer's *The Sign of Leo* was certainly written by Rohmer, but Paul Gégauff was in on the original idea and helped with the dialogue. The script for *Paris Belongs to Us*, directed by Jacques Rivette, was co-written with Jean Gruault. By contrast, Jacques Demy alone wrote the script and dialogue for *Lola*, as he did with virtually all his other movies, just as his wife Agnès Varda did for *Cléo from 5 to 7*. But, to return to one of the pillars of 1950s *Cahiers* critics, Pierre Kast's 1957 production of *Girl in his Pocket* was based on a script by France Roche, who had herself adopted the idea from a science fiction novel by Waldemar Kaempfert. For *Le Bel Âge*, a collection of three connected short stories, Kast adapted a novella by Alberto Moravia, *An Old Imbecile*, for the first episode, and co-wrote the other two tales with Jacques Doniol-Valcroze. The latter wrote and directed his own scripts for *A Game for Six Lovers* and *Coeur battant* (*The French Game*, 1961).

It thus becomes clear that the configuration hoped for by Astruc and Truffaut in their programmatic articles was far from dominant. Nonetheless, the adaptations were characterized by a much more clearly defined and active role played by the director in working out the script during the preproduction phase than had been the norm earlier for directors such as Marcel Carné, Claude Autant-Lara, and Yves Allégret. Taken together, New Wave scripts were more personal and often more autobiographical than those from the "tradition of quality." However, it was really in the *mise-en-scène*, the relation to the characters, and the serious or ironic private film references that this subjectivity was inscribed. Narration in New Wave films is rarely impersonal and this was partly what irritated critics who championed classical stories and put off those spectators who were hesitant to accept the highly obvious interventions by the auteur, except in several specific genres like burlesque or detective film parodies.

The adaptations of novels, short stories, or plays did not disappear during the New Wave, as these statistics demonstrate:

1956   Three years before the New Wave, of the 91 French films produced, 52 had original scripts, 29 were adaptations of novels or short stories, and 10 were theatrical plays.

1959   Of the 105 films, 54 had original scripts, 43 were adaptations of novels or short stories, 6 were from theatrical plays, and 2 were documentaries.

1960   Of the 123 films, 71 had original scripts, 46 were adaptations of novels and short stories, 5 were from theatrical plays, and 1 was an adapted ballet.

1961   Of the 105 films, 61 had original scripts, 38 were adaptations of novels and short stories, 4 were from theatrical plays, and 2 were inspired by comic strips.

1963   Of the 88 films, 36 had original scripts, 45 were adaptations of novels and short stories, 6 were from theatrical plays, and 1 was a remake.

The percentage of original scripts increased slightly from 1959 to 1961, but the increases were hardly significant.

Directors, producers, and writers thus continued to adapt novels, but less and less were they the sort of novels by Emile Zola and Stendhal that had typified 1950s French production. By the early 1960s, those sorts of adaptation were gradually becoming the subject-matter for television projects. There was a shift from the dominant naturalist model offered by René Clément's *Gervaise* or Yves Allégret's movies toward a model more influenced by Balzac, though it was greatly transformed by Rivette, whose *Out One*, for instance, was inspired by Balzac's *Story of 13* and *The Belle Noiseuse* by *The Unknown Masterpiece*. Truffaut and Chabrol also cite Balzac in *The 400 Blows* and *The Cousins*. The naturalist model privileged costume dramas, social class conflicts, and a strong "typage" of characters, bordering on stereotyping. The Balzacian model dealt more often with a critical description of contemporary society, underlining the contradictions that determined conflicts that were as much psychological as social.

In a certain sense, the New Wave is more a generational changing of the guard among scriptwriters than an exclusive promotion of auteur directors. The exhaustive filmographies of Paul Gégauff and Jean Gruault reveal the importance of these two auteurs in the movement's production. For example, after having worked with one of the great "masters" for New Wave filmmakers, Roberto Rossellini, Gruault collaborated on scripts with Godard (*Les Carabiniers*), Rivette (*Paris Belongs to Us, The Nun*), Truffaut (*Jules and Jim, Two English Girls, The Wild Child, The Green Room*), Alain Resnais (*My American Uncle, Life is a Novel*, and *L'Amour à mort*). Gruault offers a strong, well-documented, and quite personal account of his collaboration with Rossellini, Truffaut, Rivette, and Resnais in his book *Ce que dit l'autre* (*What the Other One Said*).[4]

The Plan-of-Action Script

In fact, it is necessary to oppose two conceptions of the script, as they have been defined by Francis Vanoye in his *Scénarios modèles, modèles de scénario*: the "program-script" (*scénario-programme*) organizes the story events into a fixed structure, ready to be filmed; the "plan-of-action script" (*scénario-dispositif*) is more open to the uncertainties of production, to chance encounters, and ideas that suddenly come to the auteur in the here and now of filming. Clearly, the plan-of-action script is the New Wave's ideal, which Godard would expand upon greatly as his career advanced.

But, although the program-script dominates "classical" cinema, it is far from absent from some New Wave films, since it governs productions by Agnès Varda, Alain Resnais, and Jacques Demy. The films of Truffaut and Chabrol oscillate from one pole to the other, though the program-script clearly dominates their output.

The plan-of-action script is an ideal that the New Wave often attempts to achieve, but it reigns supreme in the aesthetic approach of Jean Rouch and Jacques Rozier. Rouch's experiments, even those that seem less convincing in regards to their outcome, never cease to haunt the creative imagination of Godard, Rivette, and Rohmer. At the opening of *The Human Pyramid*, Rouch, seated in the grass, explains to the young students that he had gathered together that they will write the "script" at the same time as he directs it. In *Punishment*, the director "unleashes" a young actress whom he asks to play the role of a high school girl who is shut out of school one morning by her teacher and now heads off to Luxembourg Gardens where she encounters three young men hanging out there. While Godard wrote the dialogue for his characters in *All the Boys are Called Patrick* in a very personal manner, Rouch, by contrast, lets his actors improvise their lines completely. This approach is also followed by Jacques Rozier, though to a slightly lesser extent in *Adieu Philippine* than in *Du côté d'Orouet* (*Near Orouet*, 1973). Later, this manner will be adopted by Rivette for his *Céline et Julie vont en bateau* (*Céline and Julie Go Boating*, 1974) and even more radically by Rohmer in his *Le Rayon vert* (*Summer*, 1986).

It is precisely this narrative strategy that Rivette encouraged during an interview after directing *L'Amour fou*, which was a sort of manifesto for the plan-of-action script:

> Time was, in a so-called classical tradition of cinema, when the preparation of a film meant first of all finding a good story, developing it, scripting it and writing dialogue; with that done, you found actors who suited the characters and then you shot it. This is something I've done twice, with *Paris Belongs to Us*, and *The Nun*. . . . What I have tried since – after many others, following the precedents of Rouch, Godard, and so on – is to attempt to find, alone or in company (I always set out from the desire to make a film with particular actors), a generating principle which will then, as though on its own (I stress the "as though"), develop in an autonomous manner and engender a filmic product from which, afterwards, a film destined eventually for screening to audiences can be cut, or rather "produced."[5]

The dramaturgy of films directed by Rivette in *Out One* and *Céline and Julie Go Boating* springs directly from these principles, just as will his later films, from *Pont du Nord* (1981) through *Haut, bas, fragile* (*Up, Down, Fragile*, 1995).

It is within these limits of improvised fiction that the most pronounced specificity of the New Wave's creative approach is diametrically apposed to the program-script. It opens onto what, in 1960, was called "*cinéma vérité*," in regard to Rouch and Morin's *Chronicle of a Summer*. However, that film's approach proved less significant, since it defined itself within the realm of the film-inquiry rather than being a fiction film like *The Punishment*, which provided a veritable aesthetic matrix for films by Rivette and Rohmer in the 1970s and '80s.

Techniques of Adaptation, the Relation to Writing

Although they denounced a certain conception of adaptation in vogue during the 1950s, that which transformed novels by Stendhal and André Gide into ancestors of the television series, the New Wave directors did not renounce the inspiration that came from the literary sources about which they were impassioned; on the contrary. But their practice of adaptation was radically different. Most of their films did not try to hide from their literary sources and did not try to substitute visual "equivalences" for scenes considered anti-cinematic.

Two films helped show them the way: *The Silence of the Sea*, filmed by Melville who remained very faithful to the text by novelist Vercors, since the original story is also told in voice-over by the narrator (the young woman's uncle, played by Jean-Marie Robain); and *The Crimson Curtain*, adapted by Astruc from a novella by Barbey d'Aurevilly. In both these cases, though for different reasons, one of the protagonists, and both times it is a young woman, refuses to speak, and the director presents the speech from a masculine narrator who recounts the story in voice-over. Astruc, referring to his adaptation, mentioned "filming the grandeur of nature in the text," and clarified it by saying that he intended to remain scrupulously faithful to Barbey's text. Adapting *One Life*, by Maupassant, Astruc combined fragments of voice-over commentary with the voice of the heroine Jeanne (Maria Schell) to help describe her encounter with the man she will marry.

Truffaut remained faithful to the same strategy when he adapted the Maurice Pons short story for *The Mischief Makers*. Throughout this luminous short film, the external narrator's voice (from actor Michel François) recalls the exploits of the "brats" in a very elegant and literary manner, since it is the exact same text as the writer's. The film's richness resides precisely in the relation established between the nostalgic text, read *a posteriori*, and the events that we are shown in the image, accompanied occasionally by spontaneous shards of dialogue from the characters in their real southern French, Gard, dialect. Several years later, when adapting Henri-Pierre Roché, Truffaut constructed the soundtrack for *Jules and Jim* to include large segments of voice-over commentary spoken by Michel Subor (the actor from *Le Petit Soldat*) alternating with Georges Delerue's music. This verbal enunciation of the text that engulfs the filmic track is even more prominent in *Two English Girls*. In the end, it is a way for the director to offer a homage to the author he or she adapts, respecting each word of the text.

This verbal dimension will be one of the constants in the New Wave, with the director precisely citing the very text of the author being adapted. For example, there are fragments of Moravia's novel ("I often thought that Camille would leave me . . .") at the center of Godard's adaptation for *Contempt*, and he leaves an even larger space for the interior monologues when the script is original and not adapted, as in Bruno Forestier in *Le Petit Soldat*. Similarly, Rohmer's narrators in *The Girl at the Monceau Bakery* ("Paris, the Monceau intersection . . .") and *The Collector*, as well as Jean Eustache's *Le Père Noël a les yeux bleus* (*Santa Claus has Blue Eyes*, 1966), all feature commentary. At the origins of this trend there is the voice of Jean Rouch commenting on *Les Maîtres fous* (*The Crazy Masters*, 1955), or his actor Oumaraou Ganda pretending to be Edward G. Robinson in Rouch's *Me, a Black Man*.

The New Wave advanced the notion of a *mise-en-scène* of the voice. Three decades after the coming of sound, it allowed directors to exploit all the possibilities in the soundtrack, and especially speech. It offered a cinema that was not ashamed to speak, helping dismiss the out-of-date myth, imposed by theorists in the 1920s, that located the primacy of the cinema in the image. The New Wave did not hesitate to integrate songs and popular music of the time into the film, as René Clair had done in *Sous les toits de Paris* (*Under the Roofs of Paris*, 1930) and *Quatorze Juillet* (*Bastille Day*, 1933). Songs by Charles Aznavour appear in *A Woman is a Woman* and the characters dance to his "Madison" in *Band of Outsiders*, Jean Ferrat is heard in *My Life to Live*, and Boby Lapointe performs his famous "Raspberry" number in *Shoot the Piano Player*, while Serge Rezvani, a.k.a. Bassiak, sings "Le Tourbillon" with Jeanne Moreau in *Jules and Jim*.

For his part, Alain Resnais was one of the major documentary filmmakers of the 1950s, and he was a great proponent of voice-over commentary, especially in *Night and Fog*, whose text was written by Jean Cayrol and spoken by Michel Bouquet to accompany those horrible images from the archives that remain etched in our memories. Resnais would also construct the opening sequences of his first two feature films with recitative voices: Emmanuelle Riva, playing the French nurse from Nevers, speaks over the images of victims of the atomic blast in Hiroshima, while the handsome lover, played by Giorgia Albertazzi, speaks in his Italian accent as his gaze surveys the ceilings and long corridors of the hotel at Marienbad. This aesthetic direction leads to the Duras films of the 1970s, such as *La Femme de Gange* (*Woman of Ganges*, 1974) and *India Song* (1975) where her films employ voices-off from female, though anonymous, narrators.

Exiting the Studios and the Rediscovery of Location Shooting

One decisive New Wave action was to move away from studio-bound cinema. The New Wave thereby inscribed itself into a Rossellini-inspired gesture, following in the tradition of *Rome Open City* (1945), *Paisan* (1946), and *Voyage in Italy* (1953). Rossellini had presented a radically different face of Italy by showing Rome's popular neighborhoods, the landscapes of the highways, and the museums of Naples.

In *La Pointe courte*, Agnès Varda had taken the step of describing, alternately, the romantic relations of a young married couple, speaking in a very lofty, literary language, and the daily lives of fishermen, shot in the actual locations where they worked and lived. One often finds in New Wave works this *mise-en-scène* of the fiction set within real places, or, as cinematic vocabulary typically labels it, natural settings. Yet these locations are hardly chosen at random. They are places that the auteurs strode through in their youth. Their inscription contributes mightily to the autobiographical dimension of these movies.

In Louis Malle's *Elevator to the Gallows*, we can see a classical French detective film of the 1950s shot in studio sets: the interior of the elevator where the lead character is trapped and the interiors of the buildings. However, this portion of the film alternates with pre-New Wave segments that present an original description of Paris at night, its streets, telephone booths, etc., as we follow the meanderings of the woman, Florence, as she silently searches for her trapped lover, often to the wonderful, non-diegetic musical accompaniment of the Miles Davis soundtrack. Malle's model was influenced by the earlier work of Jean-Pierre Melville, who in turn built on Malle's innovations when filming Manhattan at night, where he described the same sort of action (two reporters search for a witness). Obviously, Melville traveled to New York to film on location in natural settings. The result was *Deux hommes dans Manhattan* (*Two Men in Manhattan*, 1959).

While shooting *Le Beau Serge*, Claude Chabrol and his crew stayed in the village where he spent his adolescence during four years of the Occupation, the village where he discovered the cinema, young girls, and alcoholism: "The village topography was a determining factor. I wanted the spectators to follow the actors in all their comings and goings so they would come to recognize places, alleys, and houses. To do so I exposed many miles worth of film."[6]

While, in *The Cousins*, Chabrol did go into the studio to construct the large apartment, supposedly set in the expensive Paris suburb of Neuilly, lent by Paul's (Jean-Claude Brialy) rich, ever absent anthropologist uncle and regularly used by Paul for his parties, he also filmed a great deal of the action on location in Paris. He shot in the streets, showed the Champs-Elysées being criss-crossed by Paul in his convertible, the bookstores of the Latin Quarter, the Place Edmond-Rostand, and other hangouts of the young right-wing set that held echoes of Chabrol's early days as a student. The aesthetic success of Chabrol's *The Good Girls* also depends in large part on the authenticity of the vast electric appliance store where the four young sales women are bored to death, as well as such locations as the streets at night, the Pacra concert hall, the zoo, and the swimming pool.

All the action in *The 400 Blows* is situated in the neighborhood where Truffaut spent his childhood: the 18th arrondissement and Place Clichy. In *The Soft Skin*, Truffaut even went so far as to shoot in his own apartment on rue Conseiller-Collignon to present the conjugal relations between the professor (played by Jean Desailly) and his wife (Nelly Benedetti).

Breathless serves as a veritable geographic portrait of 1959 Paris with its small tourist hotel, cafés, grand avenues like the Champs-Elysées shot near the *Cahiers du Cinéma* offices, the movie houses, hidden passageways, La Pergola brasserie in Saint-Germain-des-Prés, and the photography studio on rue Campagne-Première.

If *Le Petit Soldat* and *A Woman is a Woman* appear as such personal films, it is because the former describes Bruno Forestier in Geneva, situated in the area around Léman Lake, all places of Godard's childhood. For *A Woman is a Woman*, Godard's musical comedy in intense color, he shot his own wife, Anna Karina, in their apartment on rue du faubourg Saint-Denis. The film is a beautiful cinemascope documentary on the grand boulevards, the Saint-Denis arch, and the cafés and popular cabarets of the neighborhood. Even as abstract a fable as *Les Carabiniers*, situated in an imaginary country somewhere in the land of Ubu, gains its force from its inscription within the wasteland of Rungis and the no man's land of the area outside Paris.

The very title for Rivette's first feature, *Paris Belongs to Us*, signals its role in the same New Wave program. Rivette provides us with a survey of Paris that is quite singular, returning to the paths taken by Louis Feuillade, who filmed Paris as if it were a desert in his 1915 *Vampires*, and René Clair of *Paris qui dort* (*The Crazy Ray*, or *Paris Asleep*, 1924). We get to see the roof of the Sarah Bernhardt Theater, the rue des Cannettes, the Place Sorbonne, the Arts Bridge, a modest hotel where the American journalist fleeing McCarthyism stays, the cheaper *chambres de bonne* where the young provincial woman lives, the numerous staircases and attics of the buildings that reinforce the labyrinthian aspect of the story. Rivette's Paris is an obscure maze, where intricate conspiracies are hatched by the vague Organization, a lucid premonition of the French Organization of the Secret Army (OAS). All the characters feel threatened. The atmosphere evoked by the film recalls the American witch hunts or the Budapest revolution recently crushed by Soviet tanks, but the film also presents a fairly remarkable description of the intellectual climate of the end of the Fourth Republic, with its political and military plots concerning the Algerian War. The character of the idealist and paranoid young theatrical director (who is indeed killed by the story's end) struggles to stage his version of *Pericles* while some secret police operate in the shadows, just like in a Fritz Lang detective movie where everything is watched over by Mabuse.

With his first feature, *The Sign of Leo*, Eric Rohmer pushes even further this descriptive tendency that owes so much to documentary practice and which we find so often in New Wave films. Actually, the main character of *The Sign of Leo* is not the failed American painter and sometime bohemian played by Jess Hahn and his heavy silhouette; rather, it is the capital city in the month of August, made up of the quais along the Seine, the small Latin Quarter hotels, the métro and streets in the suburbs. Despite the commercial failure of this film, Rohmer continued to radicalize his approach as he undertook his first Moral Tales. *The Girl at the Monceau Bakery* describes in detail the neighborhood from which the bakery and the film take their name, and the film's exposition is a maniacal presentation of the urban topography where the narrator will wander. The narrator does not spare us the name of a single street, intersection, or alleyway. The subject is precisely there since it involves the path to the bakery, which is also clearly a moral journey.

A few years later, the site is an isolated villa in Ramatuelle on the Mediterranean, which shelters an art dealer on his monastic vacation. He has decided to devote himself to internal meditation, far from feminine temptation, until the inopportune meeting with a very intriguing female *Collector*.

But the film that explicitly inscribes the primacy of place is, to a certain extent, the second cinematic manifesto of the New Wave, produced by Barbet Schroeder as the movement's first phase (the period 1959–63) was ending. It was *Six in Paris*, with episodes shot by Jean Douchet, Jean Rouch, Jean-Daniel Pollet, Jean-Luc Godard, Eric Rohmer, and Claude Chabrol, all in 16 mm and released in 1965. Each of the six short films that make up *Six in Paris* emphasizes the topography of a place, with a story that derives from the structure of each featured neighborhood. The episode that remains

Rohmer offers precise time and location in *The Girl at the Monceau Bakery* (Rohmer, 1962).

Produced by Barbet Schroeder

most faithful to that program is Eric Rohmer's *Place de l'Etoile* whose tale is based in part on the non-coordination of the traffic lights that circle the Arc de Triomphe and thus govern the trajectory of the pedestrians having to cross all those streets.

Techniques of Filming

The choice of subject-matter and its integration into a natural location generated a whole series of consequences that were purely technical. New Wave films brought forth smaller production crews, often using fewer positions than those imposed by the technician unions. Hence, the strong resistance from the traditional guilds, especially the set designers and studio personnel. These tensions also motivated a discourse that was increasingly critical of the absence of professionalism, the notorious incompetence of the young directors, and the supposedly rushed, slapdash nature of their works. This discourse was unleashed in particular against Godard's earliest films, which did not hesitate to provoke spectators and critics alike. In the opening scene of *My Life to Live*, for instance, he frames an entire conversation involving a couple seated at a bar from their back.

> The New Wave is a school of critics who dare each other actually to try their hand at filmmaking. It is filmmaking to see if one is capable of filmmaking. . . . The films they have produced themselves are amateurish: films in which incompetence, if not the rule, is adopted as a feature of style. In comparison with everyday, technically over-slick productions, these slapdash films momentarily took the public by surprise – they saw in them, and rightly so, a certain quality of freshness. Once incompetence has been overcome (probably reluctantly) and replaced by virtuosity, people pretty quickly noticed in someone like Chabrol an irrevocable decline in sincerity. Once a New Wave director learns his profession properly, his breeziness misfires and becomes grotesque. Godard, at the present stage of his career [in 1962], is no longer creating cinema; moreover, he is trying very hard not to look too much as though he is.[7]

Some of the new auteurs moved in the same direction under the pretext of minimizing technique. For instance, Chabrol delighted in recalling how he had no experience from the moment he began filming *Le Beau Serge*: "Rabier [the camera operator] invited me to look through the camera's viewfinder. I got my eye in place . . . but saw nothing. Kindly, Rabier explained that I was trying to look into a bolt. . . . We fell three days behind during the first week of filming. I made every mistake possible."[8] Furthermore, Chabrol continually claimed that one could learn film technique in half a day: "Everything you need to know to direct any movie can be learned in four hours. Courses at IDHEC [the French film production school] should last only half a day."[9]

This lack of initial schooling has since been exaggerated. The most important point is that most of these directors never took conventional career paths, working their way up as assistants. Yet even this claim needs qualification. Truffaut did shoot in 16 mm, filming *A Visit*, before launching into *The Mischief Makers*. Godard, Rivette, and Rohmer had all shot films in that substandard format since the early 1950s. Godard directed a short commercial assignment, *Operation Cement*, and had collaborated on productions with Pierre Schoendoerffer, all while editing tourist films for the *Knowledge of the World* series. Jacques Rozier graduated from IDHEC, which Louis Malle also attended. Jacques Demy graduated from the Louis-Lumière School and was an assistant to animator Paul Grimault and documentarist Georges Rouquier. Agnès Varda was a professional photographer when she entered into her adventure of making *La Pointe Courte*. We could cite many more examples of similar apprenticeships.

Nevertheless, this legend reinforced the romantic myth of New Wave creation. It pleased the press, which could valorize the lack of an apprenticeship if they liked the films, or, in the opposite situation, they could cite it to help denounce these directors as imposters. But these young directors were all supported and assisted by their cinematographers, or chief camera operators. Two names in particular deserve our attention: Henri Decae and Raoul Coutard, technicians who were more open-minded than their colleagues.

Henri Decae began as a photo-journalist, then worked as a sound engineer and sound editor. He had just begun making a few short films himself when he agreed to light Jean-Pierre Melville's *Silence of the Sea*, for which he also ended up editing and mixing the sound. He collaborated again with

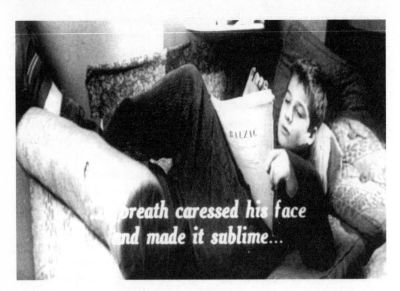

...reath caressed his face
...nd made it sublime...

Decae's interior shooting for *The 400 Blows* (Truffaut, 1959; it is an anamorphic frame of Jean-Pierre Léaud as Antoine Doinel).
Produced by Les Films du Carosse

Melville on *The Strange Ones*, but it was his distinctive camera work for *Bob le Flambeur* that caught the attention of the young critics. Louis Malle shot his first two features with Decae, then Chabrol hired him for his first three features: "For my director of photography I thought of Henri Decae since I had admired *Bob le Flambeur*. It was hard for him to find work at that point. There was something of a boycott against him because he helped on a film about the Korean War."[10]

Truffaut also hired Decae for *The 400 Blows*. His collaboration with Malle and Chabrol had now given him a very professional status, so he was the highest-paid person on this first feature by Truffaut's Films du Carrosse: "With his sharply contrasted black and white, his liking for natural lighting, and his great working speed, Decae was an ideal collaborator for Truffaut, who probably needed to feel confident on the technical level," explain Truffaut's biographers.[11] All this led Decae to work with the "grand professional" René Clément, beginning with *Plein soleil* (*Purple Noon*, 1960). Henri Decae was thus a cinematographer who was willing from the start to adapt to the most precarious and audacious conditions of production; and it was he who liberated the camera from its fixed tripod. He made the New Wave possible, backing up Melville, Malle, Chabrol, and Truffaut.

Raoul Coutard joined the French expeditionary force of the Far East in May 1945, serving five and a half years in Vietnam. Afterward, he was a war correspondent and photographer for *Paris-Match* and *Life*, as well as the magazine *Indochine Sud-Est-Asiatique*. It was in southeast Asia that he met Pierre Schoendoerffer, who hired him as camera operator for his adaptations of Pierre Loti's work, produced by Georges de Beauregard. He was thus experienced in techniques of news gathering and reporting, and forged a great mastery of hand-held camerawork while being happy to film in natural light when there was nothing else. It was de Beauregard who assigned him to Godard for *Breathless* and, to a certain extent, their meeting was providential. Coutard adapted quickly to that director's very unusual filming conditions, which increased the technical handicaps, such as filming two actors in a tiny hotel room with a minimum of light or following them along the Champs-Elysées with the camera hidden in a postal pushcart. "Godard told me to imagine I was a reporter following these people. So, I had to be light, mobile, and ready to hide when we shot in the street."[12] Raoul Coutard would go on to make a total of ten films with Godard, including *Weekend* and *Prénom Carmen* (*First Name Carmen*, 1984). He would also shoot four features by Truffaut: *Shoot the Piano Player*, *Jules and Jim*, *The Soft Skin*, and *The Bride Wore Black*. And it was Coutard who overexposed the luminous images for *Lola*, just as Jacques Demy requested.

One can argue that with the ten films he lit for Godard during the 1960s, Raoul Coutard completely revolutionized the plastic values of French cinema, changing both its lighting style and visual aesthetic. This new image was also the product of an evolution in techniques. Faster and more sensitive film stocks existed for photo journalists but not for motion picture camera operators. Thus, it had been, to use a photographic equivalent, the "Harcourt" style that dominated the visual aesthetic of French films in the 1950s.

Coutard's revolutionary "new image" for Belmondo driving in *Breathless* (Godard, 1960).
Produced by Les Films de Georges de Beauregard

In order to adapt to the aesthetic demands established by Godard, Raoul Coutard employed a new film stock, Ilford HPS, previously reserved exclusively for still photography. He used a Cameflex camera, whose perforations were closest to the Leica camera, so as to expose the 50-foot rolls, which he spliced together for his motion picture camera. At Godard's request, Coutard intervened in the development process as well, pushing the exposed stock to double its sensitivity.[13] The goals of these "brainstorms" were to be able to shoot more quickly and not have to hinder the characters' movement, all in order to capture them in their environment more successfully.

Each new film by Godard and Coutard was an original visual experience. With *Les Carabiniers*, Godard wanted to recapture a certain contrast that characterized silent cinema, so he played with different film stocks, the actors' make-up, and the processing of the archival footage that he inserted in the montages. Film reviewers had trouble understanding this approach and violently attacked the movie under the pretext of its botched and off-hand technique. Cut to the quick, Godard responded to these very cruel comments by citing all the precise techniques employed in order to prove his nearly maniacal perfectionism, right down to respecting the exact sound of the machine guns:

Jean Rochereau (of *La Croix*): There are only carelessly filmed shots, edited any old way, and laden with bad matches.

Jean-Luc Godard: We shot for four weeks during a harsh winter that encouraged us to be rigorous, and from script to mixing, everything happened under its spell. The soundtrack, in particular, thanks to engineers Hortion and Maumont, was given special attention. Each gun, each explosion was recorded separately, then remixed, even though it would have been easy to buy them from Zanuck. Each airplane possesses its own distinct engine noise, and we never put the roaring of a Heinkel for the rapid-fire bursts of a Spitfire. Much less the bursts of a Berreta when you saw a Thomson machine gun. The editing took longer than for *Breathless*, and the mixing resembled that of Resnais or Bresson. The music was recorded at the very serious Schola Cantorum. As for the mismatches, there is one that is superb, moving, Eisensteinian, in the scene where one of the shots could have been taken right out of *Potemkin*. We see an establishing shot of a non-commissioned officer in the royal army removing the cap from a young partisan woman, as blonde as the wheat of her Soviet farm. In the next shot, in close-up, we see the same gesture. And so? What is a match if not the passage from one shot to another? This shift could be made without a clash – and it is the match that is pretty much perfected over 40 years by American cinema and editors who, in detective films and comedies, and from comedies into westerns, installed and refined the principle of an accurate match on action, in the same position, so as not to break the melodic unity of the scene. In brief, a purely manual match, a process of *écriture* or discourse. But one can also shift from one shot to the next, not for a discursive reason, but for a dramatic reason, and that is the Eisenstein match, which opposes one form to another and inextricably links them by the same process. The shift from long shot to close-up becomes then that of minor to major in music, for instance, or vice versa. In brief, the match is a sort of rhyme, it is not worth starting the battle of Hernani over staircases that must be hidden. One simply needs to know when, where, and how.[14]

Godard reveals his aesthetic decisions with sufficient clarity that it is not necessary for us to summarize any further. The reference to Eisenstein, who was fundamental to the visual aesthetic of *Les Carabiniers*, highlights the rediscovery of montage that was under way by the New Wave auteurs, and especially Godard, Resnais, Rivette, and Rozier.

Montage/Editing

Editing is the technical practice most obvious to critics and spectators. It "leaps out" at us. With *Hiroshima mon amour*, Resnais bases his narrative on the discontinuity of shots, the progressive emergence of memory that appears via the brief images, and then their serial arrangement. He alternates images of the present in Hiroshima with those of the past in Nevers, France. The final portion of the film is a veritable modern musical score structured on the music of Giovanni Fusco during which the voice of Emmanuelle Riva, the traveling shots of the streets at night in the Japanese city, and the pans of the misty, grey walls of Nevers are more and more inextricably mixed. Jean-Luc Godard would prove to be one of the first to retain this lesson. With *Breathless* he destroys the rules of classical composition, and privileges syncopated editing in the action sequences (such as the car chase early in the movie), as well as during the dialogue scenes (as when Michel Poiccard comments on Patricia's neck during a car ride, edited with jumpcuts). But, heading in a completely different direction, he occasionally opts for shot sequences, either straight-on (Michel and Patricia's conversation on the Champs-Elysées) or circular (the final discussion in the apartment on rue Campagne-Première). As we have suggested, he never hesitates to extend a sequence to three or four times its traditional duration, as is the case in the central part of the film, which features a long conversation between Michel and Patricia in her room. This extension shows no concern for the conventional constraints founded on continuity editing. Those rules had become absurd. Godard breaks them with elation and thus invents modern montage by rediscovering the poetic inventions of the great montage editors of 1920s Soviet cinema.

Jumpcuts in *Breathless* (Godard, 1960; two sequential frames).
Produced by Les Films de Georges de Beauregard

But he never confines himself to a narrow rhetoric. With *Le Petit Soldat*, his innovation passes to long flash pans, rapidly reframing from one "shot" to the next, a process that, at the time, made conventional cinema technicians bristle because they belonged exclusively to the amateur cinema. In *My Life to Live*, he explores the resources available to the long take, whether mobile (Nana in her record store), or static (the scene of her writing a letter in her schoolgirl's notebook), or as lateral tracking shots (the opening discussion in the bar).

Godard is certainly the most innovative New Wave director, exploring all the possible avenues for cinematic expression. But Jacques Rivette and Jacques Rozier, each in their own manner, also base their styles on the powers of montage and discontinuity editing. Both of them recorded a great number of shots with synchronized sound and it is the editing process that organizes this abundant material, which a prior script could neither describe nor anticipate. This approach assumes a great confidence on the part of the producer, since it is often experimental and can prove expensive, especially in terms of the amount of film exposed. It also results often in works that are longer than the average screen time, going beyond the norms of commercial exhibition. The leading example of this tendency is Rivette's *L'Amour fou* (1968). It is a brilliant reworking of the structure from *Paris Belongs to Us*, on a related topic. It is based on an alternation between long takes, some in 35 mm (the developing relationships between the director, his wife, and the partners) and others in 16 mm (a television crew records the phases of the theatrical staging of *Andromache*, directed by Sebastian, played by J. P. Kalfon). Rivette pushed this experiment even further with the 12 hours and 40 minutes of *Out One* in 1971, which he reduced to a "short" version of 4 hours and 15 minutes. It was again Jean Rouch who had opened this route with his ethnographic films, such as the series *Siguis* in which he shot ceremonies of aging among the Dogons on the cliffs of Bandiagara in Mali over an eight-year period, from 1966 through 1973. Without these long films, Jean Eustache never would have tried to release *La Maman et le putain* (*The Mother and the Whore*, 1973) which ran to 3 hours and 40 minutes, composed of relatively few shots, of long duration.

But the New Wave also made innovations in the area of sound.

Synchronized Sound

⌐This aesthetic debate revolves essentially around the question of post-synchronization. One of the directors most admired by the new auteurs was Jean Renoir. Yet he had very personal views regarding sound recording and dialogue. From 1930 on, Renoir was an unconditional partisan of "direct sound," or sound recorded during the filming process⌐ This practice was particularly difficult to accomplish in those days of optical sound recording, which was a heavy, constrictive process that greatly limited the options available for mixing. But Renoir, intractable on this point, preferred to sacrifice the precision of sound quality for its authenticity. Since his *On purge bébé* (*Baby Gets a Laxative*, 1931) and especially *La Chienne* (*The Bitch*, 1931), he recorded the sound for his films with the "direct" method. However, he was one of very few directors to do so, though Marcel Pagnol followed the same procedure.

⌐During the 1950s, despite the widespread use of magnetic sound recording, which offered many new possibilities, the practice of post-synchronization reigned supreme as the standard technique. Furthermore, by the end of that decade, direct sound still posed cumbersome and difficult conditions for recording dialogue (to say nothing of the need for more retakes), all of which ran counter to the needs set by the small budgets of the New Wave. Which helps explain why the first films by Chabrol, Truffaut, Godard, Rivette, and Rohmer were post-synchronized. Some of these, such as *Breathless*, were even shot like completely silent movies without any wild "guide tracks," to record the dialogue spoken on the set as a guide for use later in duping.⌐

Aside from Renoir, one other director became a reference point, especially to Jean-Luc Godard, who was a particularly fervent admirer. It was, once again, Jean Rouch. He had shot short ethnographic films in 16mm since the late 1940s, which he usually post-synchronized because of his lack of adequate technical equipment. But in 1958 he began his production of *Me, a Black Man*, a semi-improvised fiction film performed by African actors; Rouch then asked these actors to dupe quite freely over their own performances. This duping was even recorded in a radio studio.[15] Godard was enthralled by the freedom of the interior monologues by the central protagonist as well as by the emotional effectiveness of the post-synchronization of these very random comments. He would be inspired by Rouch's approach, first in post-synchronizing *Charlotte and Her Jules*, where he had the audacity to dupe in Jean-Paul Belmondo's dialogue himself, and then in *Breathless*, where the same liberty and offhandedness are obvious. With *Le Petit Soldat* and *A Woman is a Woman*, Godard continued his experiments with post-synchronization. For the former, he launched a sort of personal diary in interior voice; in total contrast, for the latter, the colorful cinemascope comedy, he multiplied the musical and vocal refrains, helped by a particularly creative musical score by Michel Legrand.

But during this period, technological innovations caught up with creative experimentation. The synchronization of image and sound became simpler thanks to new tape recorders, such as the Nagra. These technical advances were being exploited by television and documentary cinema. It was again Rouch who pointed the way by directing *Chronicle of a Summer*, along with sociologist Edgar Morin; this feature-length inquiry became the manifesto of "*cinéma vérité*." Shot in 35 mm with a lightweight camera, the film was quite obviously recorded with direct sound. As soon as he could, Godard transposed this direct sound approach, beginning with *My Life to Live* which became in some aspects an "investigative film" aimed at the life of a Parisian prostitute. Following this film, he directed all his features with direct sound and this strategy became inseparable from his approach to "sound directing."

This search for authenticity and freer movements for the actors found its most successful realization in the first feature by Jacques Rozier, who was the most direct disciple of Jean Renoir's cinema. In *Adieu Philippine*, the New Wave found the naturalist masterpiece that the young critics at *Cahiers du Cinéma* had dreamed about. And yet, the film had to be post-synchronized by Rozier even though he had employed direct sound to record everything at the time of the filming. The sound obtained, recorded under makeshift conditions with a portable tape recorder, was not sufficiently audible, to say nothing of being in sync. Because the dialogue was largely improvised by the three young, non-professional actors, Rozier had

Three lead actors chat spontaneously in *Adieu Philippine* (Rozier, 1962).
Produced by Rome Paris Films, Unitec-Alpha, and Euro International Films

to transcribe completely the recorded material and then undertake a very long post-synchronization, as well as the very difficult editing job, all of which was further complicated by the vast amounts of film exposed and audiotape recorded during production.[16]

Thus, some of the major films in the history of cinematic form came about under particularly difficult conditions. Such was the case with *Adieu Philippine*, which was distributed three years after its production began. Filming began on August 7, 1960, but was not finished until January 1962. It premiered on September 25, 1963 at the famous La Pagode cinema in Paris, but only received a very mediocre box office return. Nonetheless, Rozier's film had a considerable influence on the aesthetic evolution of French cinema. This commercial failure derailed Rozier's subsequent career as a motion picture director. He did not direct another feature until 1970, when he shot *Near Orouet*, but this time he filmed in 16 mm with perfectly synchronized sound.

Chapter Five

New Themes and New Bodies: Characters and Actors

T HE NEW WAVE FILMS would not have found such a positive critical and popular response if they had not broached new themes or represented French society in a manner so different from previous cinematic practice. It is obviously absurd to try to define, in only a few pages, the common themes of directors who themselves described their oeuvres as personal modes of production. There are as many diverse fictional universes as there are auteur directors. We can nonetheless offer several common points that were isolated by critics at the time as representative, "brand name images" of the movement. It will become clear that these shared traits only involve the most external aspects of these films, and some are even found in the most trivial movies, such as *Le Bel Âge* or *A Game for Six Lovers*, which exist now as symptoms rather than important works. Yet, these traits also correspond closely to the New Wave as seen by its detractors, and this is why it is important here to confront those obvious themes, even if only briefly. If the New Wave had been limited to only these films, it would never have influenced cinema history as it did.

"Marivaudage and Saganism": From Astruc to Kast to Doniol-Valcroze[1]

Jacques Siclier, writing his "on the spot" assessment of the New Wave in 1960, goes back to *Bad Encounters*, adapted from a novel by Cécil Saint-Laurent. Astruc's film describes the adventure of two young provincials (played by Giani Esposito and Anouk Aimée) who come to Paris to try to launch their careers as journalists, and get their names in the papers. In his memoirs, Astruc later summarized the tale as, "A meditation on the discovery of Paris by two ambitious provincials, their joyous successes, and a portrait of a young woman of our time, who is fragile but determined."[2] The young man quickly abandons his struggle after having several articles refused. He takes the train back home to the provinces. His more ambitious friend stays behind, and after an affair with the editor of a large Paris newspaper (Jean-Claude Pascal), becomes the fashion writer, and eventually she herself becomes regularly featured in the papers. Siclier correctly observes: "Astruc's admiration for Balzac turns the movie into a sort of modern version of *Lost Illusions*."[3] Careerists succeed while idealists fail. To a certain extent, Paul Gégauff and Claude Chabrol forge the same moral lesson in *The Cousins*, where they show a serious student failing while the partying dandy passes his law exams.

However, it is noteworthy that Siclier's account of *Bad Encounters* fails to mention one of Astruc's important narrative tactics, which is to have the story told in flashback by the young woman who is now accused of having an abortion. We find her, at the beginning of the film, at the Quai des Orfèvres, being interrogated by an investigator (Yves Robert) who wants her to reveal the name of her doctor. The latter, played by Claude Dauphin, eventually kills himself. The theme of abortion will also turn up, in a much more cynical context, in *The Cousins*.

But Siclier emphasizes that the intellectual center for *Bad Encounters* is situated in Saint-Germain-des-Prés, while its social milieu is that of mainstream journalism centered around the Champs-Elysées. According to Siclier, it is from these limited worlds that the New Wave develops its universe. He lists the privileged locales of the young directors: the Latin Quarter with its students (*The Cousins*, *All the Boys are Called Patrick*, *Breathless*) and artists (*The Sign of Leo*), the business world of the Champs-Elysées (*Elevator to the Gallows*), the bourgeois neighborhood of the 16th arrondissement (*The Lovers*, *Le Bel Âge*), and Saint-Germain-des-Près (*Le Bel Âge* again). We could add areas in the provinces where the bourgeoisie had their country homes or took vacations: the chateau at Roussillon (*A Game for Six Lovers*), Alpine ski resorts at Megève (*Le Bel Âge* and

Moreau and Bory share a tub in *The Lovers* (Malle, 1958; anamorphic image).
Produced by Les Nouvelles Editions de Films

Dangerous Liaisons 1960), and, of course, the small southern port of Saint-Tropez (*Le Bel Âge, And God Created Woman,* and Marcel Moussy's *Saint-Tropez Blues,* 1961).

With *The Lovers,* the greatest box office success of the young French cinema, Louis Malle adapted a novel with Louise de Vilmorin to present the haute bourgeoisie of Paris and Dijon. He pairs the boredom felt by the heroine (Jeanne Moreau) at the horse track in the exclusive Paris suburb of Auteuil, where she meets her lover, with the rural country house in Burgundy, where she and her husband and daughter live. But then she meets a young man (Jean-Marc Bory) who drives a cheap little 2 CV car, she is struck with an erotic lightning bolt, and the two experience the famous night of lovemaking that made the movie so controversial.[4]

This human geography for the New Wave does exist. However, it is only representative of some of the more superficial films. Truffaut, Godard, some Chabrols, Rivette, but also Rouch, Rozier, Demy, and Varda offer completely different aspects of French society. One could even argue that with his *The Collector*, Rohmer wanted, not without irony, to get even with the caricatured representation of a certain sort of New Wave – the "St. Tropezian" version – with its art-gallery owners on vacation and its dandy fascinated by the most radical asceticism: "Now all that mattered for me was to read morning in its truest sense, and to associate it, like the quasi-totality of all beings on earth . . . with the idea of awakening and beginning," confides *The Collector*'s sententious narrator, Adrien.

François Truffaut, interviewed by Louis Marcorelles in October 1961, provided a very lucid view of the New Wave's limitations:

> We believed that everything had to be simplified so we could work freely and make humble films on simple subjects, hence the quantity of New Wave pictures whose only common feature is a sum of rejections – the rejection of extras, of theatrical intrigue, costly sets, explanatory scenes; these films often have three or four characters and very little action. Unfortunately, the linearity of these films ties in with a literary genre that very much annoys the critics and the first-run public right now, a genre that we might call "Saganism": sports cars, bottles of scotch, short-lived love affairs, etc. The deliberate lightness of these films passes for frivolity – sometimes wrongly, sometimes rightly. The confusion lies in that the qualities of this new cinema – gracefulness, lightness, a sense of propriety, elegance, a quick pace – parallel its faults – frivolity, lack of thought, naiveté.[5]

Two films in particular condense these conventional representations: *Le Bel Âge* by Pierre Kast and *A Game for Six Lovers* by Jacques Doniol-Valcroze. It is revealing, but also paradoxical, that both films were written and directed by two *Cahiers* critics who were older than Chabrol, Godard, and Truffaut, from a more classical cultural background, great specialists in eighteenth-century French literature, and friends of screenwriter Roger Vailland. The latter collaborated on the script for Roger Vadim's *Dangerous Liaisons 1960*, a modern version of the Laclos novel, situating the action around the 16th arrondissement in Passy, and also the French Alps at Megève.

Kast and Doniol-Valcroze's movies have in common the theme of "marivaudage," the seductive relations between intellectuals and beautiful women. The three stories assembled by Kast for *Le Bel Âge* accumulate clichés and transport the characters from an art gallery and bookstore in the 16th arrondissement to Deauville and then to Saint-Tropez and finally skiing at Megève. Kast's ambition is huge, since he wants to propose new relations between the sexes where women can take the initiative in seduction just as much as men. But, his project falls flat because of his impoverished direction of the actors and the weakness of the dialogue. Doniol-Valcroze's goals for *A Game for Six Lovers* are no more modest, since he tries to direct a modern version of *Rules of the Game* crossed with Ingmar Bergman's *Smiles of a Summer Night* (1955).

> Four characters (two women, two men), young, attractive, and rich, search for one another, tease and chase one another in the moonlight, in a universe full of seductive touching, languid looks, mussed beds, and an overly comfortable interior of a chateau. At midnight, one plays "Jesus, Joy of Man's Desiring"; in the afternoon another reads Kafka aloud on the patio. They also play jazz records, drink whiskey, and dance in the rain while the valet courts the tease of a kitchen maid.[6]

The bourgeois young people and their servants created by Doniol-Valcroze have all the depth of creatures from photo-romans; they wander through the settings without really existing. The couple formed by the butler and the maid (Michel Galabru and Bernadette Lafont) are presented with a heaviness that is meant to be contrasted with the natural elegance of their masters, but the latter ("represented by" Alexandra Stewart, Françoise Brion, Jacques Riberolles, and Paul Guers) resemble mannequins more than film characters. The only undeniable triumph of the film remains the film's title song, "L'Eau à la bouche," by Serge Gainsbourg.

If *Le Bel Âge* had little success at the box office, *A Game for Six Lovers* had much more luck, in part because, despite its weaknesses and clichés, it offered a "torrid atmosphere," opening up somewhat the representation of sexual desire on the movie screen, which was a theme common to many New Wave films and at the heart of their attraction for many student-aged spectators. Moreover, *A Game for Six Lovers* was forbidden to anyone under the age of 16 in France, which lent it more notoriety. It would be a grave historical injustice to reduce the New Wave to the presentation of seductive men in sports cars, drinking whiskey, and chasing beautiful women, with no professional concerns. Yet, this is precisely the error committed by the New Wave's principal French historians, Jacques Siclier (in 1960), Raymond Borde, and later Francis Courtade and Freddy Buache.

The Universe of the Auteurs

A quick look at Chabrol, Truffaut, and Godard, among others, clearly shows a different New Wave.

Claude Chabrol's students and salesgirls

Claude Chabrol's famous *The Cousins* is rightly important because of its great success, but also because it helped put in place a certain mythology of the New Wave that would be popularized by the mainstream press. In *The Cousins*, Chabrol, aided by his dialogue writer Paul Gégauff, offers an unusually cynical description of bohemian student life among children of the new bourgeoisie. Paul (brilliantly played by Jean-Claude Brialy) accommodates his provincial cousin, the naive Charles (Gérard Blain, used against character here), in an apartment owned by his absent uncle Henry, and furnished with guns, hunting trophies, and toy soldiers. Chabrol and Gégauff respond to the clichés developed by Marcel Carné in *The Cheats*, which offered a highly artificial treatment of spoiled 1950s youth with their wild parties and "truth or dare" games. If Chabrol and Gégauff found the mark, it was because they relied upon their memories of their own student days at law school, which they recreate with great gusto and provocative performances. There is the character of Clovis (Claude Cerval), a parasite in his 40s, and a great celebration in the apartment which features entertainment, including the strongman breaking out of chains, and Paul's candle-lit Wagnerian recitation of a Goethe poem. Brialy, and especially Cerval, continually play their parts over the top, but their overacting perfectly suits their parodic characters who are always performing. The irony in *The Cousins* transforms it into a second-degree manifesto. Hence the misunderstanding at the time with regard to the political reading of the film, which deliberately plays with the *mise-en-scène* of a "nazi carnival," and veritable *Harakiri*

Audran and Lafont, two of Chabrol's "types" in *The Good Girls* (Chabrol, 1960).
Produced by Paris Film Productions and Panitalia

puppets; critics attributed the discourse of the characters, ironic and caricatured as it was, to the auteurs, Chabrol and Gégauff.

In *The Good Girls* the same pair of auteurs describe the ennui of four
young saleswomen in an electric appliance store near the Bastille. But
mostly, Chabrol and Gégauff are interested in the psychological and emotional alienation of the characters, who are divided into four different types
(performed by Bernadette Lafont, Stéphane Audran, Clotilde Joanno, and
Lucille Saint-Simon). The film proposes a terrifying representation of men:
two vulgar men on the prowl, a naive young soldier, a son of a ridiculously
pretentious upper-middle-class family, and a sadistic motorcyclist. It is a
vitriolic portrait of romance magazines, and goes further than Federico
Fellini's *Nights of Cabiria* (1957), one of Chabrol's influences. The *Harakiri*
mood and dark humor, which anticipate the later farces of Jean-Pierre
Mocky and Bertrand Blier, revolted critics in 1960. Chabrol's movie was
far ahead of the evolution of moral values. Even more, *The Good Girls*

presented a milieu very different from the dominant world of the "germano-pratine" New Wave. This would also be the case for *The 400 Blows*, *Adieu Philippine*, and especially *Lola*.

Truffaut's childhood

Chabrol drew upon his past student days to write his first two features. Truffaut was inspired by his childhood. In the short story by Maurice Pons, used for *The Mischief Makers*, Truffaut found themes close to his own deep preoccupations. *The 400 Blows*, however, with the creation of the character Antoine Doinel, would to a certain degree inaugurate a double image of the auteur, who would pursue a fictional, cinematic biography throughout his career, going on to shoot *Antoine and Colette*, *Stolen Kisses*, *Bed and Board*, and *Love on the Run* (1979). The character of Doinel even exceeded Truffaut's oeuvre, since the same actor, Jean-Pierre Léaud, turns up as a Godardian hero in *Masculine-Feminine* and *La Chinoise*, roles that can easily be seen as extensions of those in Truffaut's films. The same is true of Léaud's appearance as Alexandre in Jean Eustache's *The Mother and the Whore*.

But *The 400 Blows* also serves as a matrix figure, since one can easily connect the film to *The Wild Child* and *Small Change*, which are new variations on the relations between adults and children and the role of education. Truffaut's Adele H. is almost like Antoine's sister, enclosed within the intransigence of her ideals. Moreover, Claude, the young man in love with both Anne and Muriel in *Two English Girls*, seems like a brother (and for good reason) to Antoine; Claude too is played by Léaud.

All of Truffaut's male characters remain eternal adolescents, especially Charlie Kohler (alias Edouard Saroyan), the timid pianist of *Shoot the Piano Player*, Bertrand Morane, "the man who loved women," and Julien Davenne, the obituary columnist who lives in a cult of the dead in *The Green Room*. The fetishism evident in these characters, especially their relation to writing and women, makes them variations on cinéphilia as obsessive neuroticism, another trait of Truffaut's universe and, more generally, of New Wave films.[7]

The different faces of Jean-Luc Godard

Even though Patrick, the high-school-aged flirt and pathological liar of *All the Boys are Called Patrick*, was conceived by Eric Rohmer, and Michel Poiccard of *Breathless* came from François Truffaut (who had named him Lucien in the original script), it is clear that both of these characters were already Godardian heros. Patrick, to whom Brialy lends his gift of the gab, is an untiring chatterbox, chasing after young women students in Luxembourg Gardens. He is a *cinéphile*, citing Mizoguchi and Kurosawa, and already referring to old Bugatti. The young blonde in short hair (Anne Colette), with whom he first flirts, dresses in striped t-shirts: she is the first incarnation of *Breathless*'s Patricia Franchini; she listens to pop music on her transistor ("Casanova, Casanova . . .") and covers the walls of her student room with pictures of James Dean and Marilyn Monroe. Patrick next takes on the face of Jean-Paul Belmondo (and the voice of Godard) in *Charlotte and Her Jules*, and he is even more talkative, boastful, and manipulative, skipping from one topic to another. This masculine verbal deluge will characterize Michel Poiccard as well as Bruno Forestier in *Le Petit Soldat*, though the latter is more taciturn. Via his dialogue, Godard completely destroys the notion of the cinematic character, transforming each male instead into a sort of mouthpiece for the director.

From the outset, *Breathless*'s Poiccard is pretty much a marginal person, vaguely a "former steward on Air France," now connected to the Parisian milieu of blackmail (his friend Tolmatchoff, the photographer Carl Zumbart) and several gangsters right out of *Bob le Flambeur*. He is a "new romantic," as Georges Sadoul observed, a 1960s face on a poetic realist hero similar to those that Carné-Prévert held so dear. Like Jean Gabin in *Quai des brumes* (*Misty Wharf*, 1938) and *Le Jour se lève* (*Daybreak*, 1939), he is tracked by the police, but Poiccard only cares about reaching his short-term goal: sleeping with the woman he loves. With *Breathless*, Godard covers much of film history integrating the legacy of the small-budget "B-movies," such as detective films from Monogram Pictures, like *Gun Crazy* (Joseph E. Lewis, 1950), with the completely heterogeneous model offered by Jean Rouch's *Me, a Black Man*. Godard's film is a sort of long monologue in which the hero tries desperately to communicate with Patricia, the young American who has trouble following his slang-filled meanderings, his literary references, anecdotes, and aphorisms. Only a bullet in the back silences him, though in the last shot he murmurs, "That's really disgusting," which the cruel police inspector Vital repeats to Patricia, as, "He said you really are a bitch." Then she adopts Michel's trademark gesture by dragging her thumb across her lips.

Even though later it was partly disowned by its director, *Breathless* retains the same impact 40 years after its release, which had transformed it into a film manifesto for the New Wave in 1960. But Godard's next few films were just as inventive, even though they were quite different from one another. *Le Petit Soldat* is structured around a long interior monologue accompanied by a somber piano score from Maurice Le Roux. The cinematic gangsters (American or Melvillean, as they are) here become extreme right-wing secret agents out to liquidate pacifist intellectuals in favor of peace in Algeria. The latter are considered antagonists to their nation, living though they are in the neutral territory of Switzerland, the land of Godard's second citizenship.

A Woman is a Woman is a magnificent declaration of love to Angela (Anna Karina), and all the young male spectators were ready to substitute themselves for Emile (Jean-Claude Brialy) to satisfy her sudden demand to become pregnant. As Angela sings, recalling Lola in *The Blue Angel* (von Sternberg, 1930), "Everyone asks why . . . I am so cruel . . . its because I'm very beautiful." It is truly regrettable that the spectators of the "nudie" pictures in Paris at that time were so desensitized to these Godardian innovations.

Paradoxically, his more popular next feature, *My Life to Live*, was also much more demanding of its spectator with its Jansenist martyrdom of a poor record store's salesgirl driven into prostitution. Nana, the main character's saga is told in 12 chapters, and in one she even receives a philosopher's lecture on language. Yet this difficult movie satisfied its audience's expectations much more strongly than did *A Woman is a Woman*. As Luis Buñuel said, not without bitter irony in regard to his own adaptation of Joseph Kessel's novel, "*Belle de jour* was perhaps the biggest commercial success of my life, a success I attribute to the hookers in my movie rather

107

Michel Poiccard (Belmondo) is recognized by Godard in *Breathless* (Godard, 1960).
Produced by Les Films de Georges de Beauregard

Karina in *My Life to Live* (Godard, 1962).
Produced by Films de la Pléïade

than to my work."[8] The subject-matter for *My Life to Live* may have had much to do with its success as well.

A New Generation of Actors

The themes and discourses from the New Wave films doubtless only partially explain the new public's strong enthusiasm during the first season or two. The adolescents who began to replace the more traditional audiences and families on Saturday evenings came to admire the new bodies of young actors who were frequently disrobed, though still in a rather modest way, by these young auteurs.

French "quality" cinema was a cinema directed by men in their 50s, and sometimes even their 70s, and it did not know how to renew the "human cattle" represented in their work, to use Alfred Hitchcock's famous expression for actors. Jean Gabin, who had been the top star of the famous French Popular Front movies 20 years earlier, was now, in 1959, 55 years old. Only Gérard Philipe, with the success of *Le Diable au corps* (*The Devil in the Flesh*, Autant-Lara, 1946), had managed to carry the weight of the new emotional needs of the young audience on his frail shoulders. However, by the 1950s he had provided a very theatrical and declamatory style that was far removed from the contemporary Hollywood school of the Actor's Studio featured in movies by Elia Kazan (*Baby Doll*, 1956) and Nicholas Ray (*Rebel Without a Cause*, 1955). Moreover, Philippe died in 1959, at the age of 37, the very year that Chabrol's and Truffaut's first features were released, leaving his final roles as Valmont in Roger Vadim's *Dangerous Liaisons, 1960* and the idealistic Mexican in Buñuel's *The Temperature Rises at El Pao* (released in 1960).

This relative absence of new actors and styles certainly explains some of the emotional hysteria displayed by critics such as Truffaut and Godard when confronted with *And God Created Woman*, a film whose scenario, written by Roger Vadim, was actually fairly conventional. What they admired, at the moment the movie hit the screens, was Brigitte Bardot's acting, or rather absence of an acting style. They were won over by her spontaneity, her manner of speaking, walking, smiling, washing her bare feet and, of course, kissing and wrapping herself freely around her male counterparts (whose physical performance was far below the level of sensuality offered by Bardot's Juliette). Brigitte Bardot, whose eventual filmography was rather mediocre and only rarely crossed paths with the New Wave, did receive a chance to interpret Camille in Godard's only international big budget movie, *Contempt*. Godard used the actress's mythical stature much more intelligently than Louis Malle could manage in *Vie privée* (*A Private Life*, 1962), the fictional biography dedicated to Bardot.

Within the New Wave proper, Bardot had only one rival of nearly equal mythic proportions: Jeanne Moreau. Moreau was the heroine of *Elevator to the Gallows*, the bourgeois wife who discovers passion in *The Lovers*, and the even more luminous Catherine who does not want to choose between Jules and Jim; she wants them both. (The conventions of the time dictated that she would have them one after the other; the era of films such as *Les*

Opening of *Elevator to the Gallows* (Malle, 1957).
Produced by Les Nouvelles Editions de Films

Valseuses (*Going Places*, Blier, 1973) had not yet arrived.) Louis Malle, an intelligent producer, but an uneven auteur, united both Bardot and Moreau in a pseudo-feminist, Mexican pseudo-western, *Viva Maria* (1965), but again, his project was less than successful.

With the notable exception of Agnès Varda, the New Wave was a movement of masculine auteurs. In contrast to the failed efforts of some 1950s commercial filmmakers, the New Wave managed to impose upon many young male actors to stand in for Michel Auclair, Daniel Gélin, and Georges Marchal who had all been discovered by Clouzot, Becker, and Henri Decoin. Alexandre Astruc played an important role in this transition. He used a male actor who was very much from the "French quality" school, the handsome Jean-Claude Pascal, but then he offered the opposite female role to the frail Anouk Aimée, which proved an inspiring move for the New Wave. However, Jean-Claude Pascal was still too handsome, with a physique corresponding to the norms of decorative classicism. Astruc was more fortunate when he borrowed Christian Marquand from Roger Vadim to play a sort of man of the woods, hunter and predator, who brutalizes the mawkish Maria Schell character in *One Life*, cited earlier. Astruc also did a remarkable job directing two "classical" actors, Daniel Gélin and Annie Girardot, but imposing a sort of Antonioni style upon them, in his *La Proie pour l'ombre* (*The Prey for the Shadow*, 1960).

As mentioned above, what proved fatal aesthetically for the films of Pierre Kast and Jacques Doniol-Valcroze was the weakness with which their actors were directed. Admittedly, their actresses were incredibly beautiful, as were the young fellows trying to seduce them. It is easy for the audience to admire the obvious charms of Alexandra Stewart, Françoise Brion, Françoise Prévost, and Ursula Kubler, as well as Gianni Esposito, Jacques Riberolles, or even Doniol-Valcroze himself. But our relations with them remain distant, all surface-level, as if we were paging through an album of fashion photos. They never had the same sort of screen presence we see demonstrated by the actors in the films of Chabrol, Truffaut, Godard, Rivette, Rohmer, or, especially, Jacques Rozier. Sometimes, the same actors were even used by both groups, as when Jean-Claude Brialy appears in *Le Bel Âge*, or when Giani Esposito went from the role of Alexandre, the Iranian prince in Jean Renoir's *French Cancan* (1955), to the unhappy lover in Kast's *Le Bel Âge*, to the tormented director in Jacques Rivette's *Paris Belongs to Us*.

The founding trio

Beginning with *The Mischief Makers* and *Le Beau Serge*, the couple Bernadette Lafont and Gérard Blain proved their ease and presence on the screen. Gérard Blain was noticed by Truffaut as the son and partner of the restaurateur played by Jean Gabin in *Voici le temps des assassins* (*Twelve Hours to Live* (UK)/*Deadlier than the Male* (USA)). Impressed, Truffaut offered Blain the role of the athletic young fiancé in *The Mischief Makers*. Blain's next role, that of a rural alcoholic, the title character for *Le Beau Serge*, suited him less well, but in Chabrol's second feature, *The Cousins*, he was perfect as the studious, inhibited student from the provinces. He rapidly moved through the New Wave before incarnating the touchy "Frenchman," who was also a good shot and rival to the pretty but dumb Germanic Hardy

Blain and Lafont in *The Mischief Makers* (Truffaut, 1957).
Produced by Les Films du Carosse

Kruger in Howard Hawks's *Hatari* (1962). Dissatisfied with his acting career, Blain devoted himself to directing courageous, personal films, distinguished by their Bressonian aesthetic.

Blain's acting partner, Jean-Claude Brialy, like Jean-Pierre Léaud and Jean-Paul Belmondo, was a real "New Wave type" actor. Brialy shifted easily and quite casually from Godard (*All the Boys are Called Patrick*, *A Story of Water*, *A Woman is a Woman*) to Chabrol (*Le Beau Serge*, *The Cousins*, where he played one of his most emblematic roles as Paul, and *The Wise Guys*), though he was a bit less at ease in Alexandre Astruc's *Sentimental Education* (1961), in which he lent his frame to Frederic Moreau in an unconvincing, modernized adaptation written by Roger Nimier. He was even in Truffaut's *The Bride Wore Black*, where his exuberance seemed a bit misplaced. Rohmer, however, exploited Brialy's natural self-satisfaction to great success in *Claire's Knee*. Brialy's Paul in *The Cousins* found a remarkable echo in his Emile of *A Woman is a Woman*, in which he played a bookstore employee who is a fan of soccer matches and detective novels, and an expert on French grammar, but is not ready to handle fatherhood. Later, Brialy directed what had been a dream project of Eric Rohmer's, *Les Malheurs de Sophie* (*Sophie's Misfortunes*, 1980), but unfortunately it lacked the right amount of sentiment and even perversion.

A hooligan becomes a priest

The more representative masculine faces of the New Wave belonged to Jean-Paul Belmondo and Jean-Pierre Léaud. Their significance is due to the sound of their voices and their diction, but their acting style is particularly indebted to Jean-Luc Godard's direction.

When he agreed to accept the role proposed by Godard for his first feature, Belmondo had already performed in nine features and a number of short films. While he only played secondary roles in *The Cheats* and *Un drôle de dimanche* (*A Strange Sort of Sunday*, Marc Allégret, 1958), he had played the lead in *Copains de dimanche* (*Sunday Buddies*, 1956), which was produced and directed by Henri Aisner, under very amateurish conditions that were similar to Chabrol's initial films, but Aisner's movie was never even distributed. That role was much closer to his eventual part in Chabrol's *À double tour*, where Belmondo, as Lazlo Kovacs, plays a parasitical friend to the son of a wealthy family. But opposite Jean Seberg, Belmondo's strengths as an actor, including his nonchalance, ease, and cynicism, were revealed by Godard. He displayed none of the physical attributes of more conventional leading men, such as Jacques Charrier; rather, his provocative virility corresponded more to the tastes of the epoch. Belmondo showed extraordinary spontaneity in the opening scene, in which he steals the car, as well as in the demanding long sequence in Patricia's room at the Sweden Hotel, where, as Michel, her rather boorish lover, he at one point exclaims to her, "I always fall for the girls who aren't made for me . . . Why don't you take your clothes off?"

What was most profoundly novel in Godard's direction was that the camera never stops following the actors; it reframes for every movement, gesture, or grimace. *Breathless* thus became a sort of documentary on the performance of the actors, and that is precisely what gave such surprising force to the characters. Belmondo, following Godard's instructions, was allowed to do anything: He addresses the spectator, hums along with the radio, insults the women hitchhikers, steals money from a former girlfriend, asks Patricia in public why she does not wear a bra, and even requests whether he can piss in her sink. All of these everyday, trivial details, previously excluded from movie screens, helped enrich the characterization, anchoring the film in the real experience of the 1960s spectator. Such behavior is also one of the reasons behind the great success of *Breathless* at the time, while it also helped motivate some violent reactions from hostile critics, as can be seen in these responses from Raymond Borde and Robert Benayoun:

> *Breathless* is a portrait, and a sympathetic one at that, of a little jerk. It is the 1960 version of *Roi des resquilleurs* [*King of the Gate Crashers*, Devaivre, 1945]. . . . Some call it anarchist. What a joke! [Belmondo as Michel] has included a few gags that assure him a reputation for casualness: lifting a skirt in the street, refusing to offer a light, blowing up at a cab driver. But it goes no further than that. He likes the police, he says it and insists on it, even as the police hunt him down; he finds that society works just fine: everything is in order, all in its place. He resembles a parachutist on leave: his exaggerated tough exterior, his thick stupidity, and also a vague anxiety of being released among the civilians; he is the trooper who feels alone, far from his unit. There is indeed a bit of soldier in this character, and, under the mask of a schemer, the deep respect of the established order. This character does not concern me at all. But he was a hit. Why? To begin with, because dummies have found a hero who fits their pitiful dreams: eternal rascals, they recognized someone they can never be, the scoundrel, and I'll bet the grocery boys felt a shudder of envy seeing him steal cars with such nonchalance. In addition, Belmondo offers the image of a certain spinelessness, fitting for his era. Schemer, relaxed, provocateur, he is nervous, hunted, and conformist. . . . Now a word regarding Jean Seberg. You cannot simultaneously give and take, says the old expression. Here we are shown a woman who is not one, but a sort of strained young man. Belmondo torments an anti-woman, which leads to many of the sexual audacities claimed by the film. Here too, Godard has cheated.[9]

Godard, to save an unprojectable film [*Breathless*], chopped it up haphazardly, counting on his potential to astonish the critics, who were not disappointed, and helped launch a new style – that of the poorly made movie. An impenitent waster of film stock, author of stupid, despicable statements on torture and denunciations, and self-promoter, Godard represents the worst regression within the French cinema, toward an intellectual illiteracy and plastic bluff.[10]

The success of *Breathless*, which was as grand as it was unexpected, immediately yielded star status to Belmondo, who then began making movies one after the other, including avant-garde productions such as Peter Brooks's adaptation of Marguerite Duras's novel *Moderato Cantabile* (1960), as well as much more commercial ventures, such as *Un singe en hiver* (*A Monkey in Winter*, Henri Verneuil, 1961) and *Cartouche* (*Swords of Blood*, Philippe de Broca, 1962). Belmondo's palette proved vast, since he was able to interpret, in very credible fashion, a priest in Melville's *Leon Morin, Priest*, as well as a young Italian peasant in love with a prostitute (*La Viaccia* (*The Love Makers*), Bolognini, 1961), a young, outraged idealist (*La Ciocciara* (*Two Women*), De Sica, 1961), and a more appropriate anarchist thief (*Le Voleur* (*The Thief of Paris*), Malle, 1966). He would return to Godard two more times: first, in a more low-key role, as Alfred in *A Woman is a Woman*, a character sacrificed a bit to the central couple played by Brialy and Anna Karina; then, five years after his role as Michel Poiccard, he played the most remarkable role of his life, as Ferdinand Griffon, the title character of *Pierrot le fou*: "My name is not Pierrot, I'm called Ferdinand," he keeps explaining. In that film he is in love with Marianne (Karina again) and an admirer of the art critic Elie Faure ("Vélasquez, after 50 years, never again painted a solid object. He wandered around things with the air and twilight").

François Truffaut used Belmondo, out of character, in *The Mississippi Mermaid* (1968) where he was Louis Mahé, a rich, rather naive fellow with a huge inheritance, a virgin, up against Catherine Deneuve as Marion, a temptress and a thief. Chabrol took fewer risks in giving him the long-awaited role as Dr Popaul in *High Heels* (1972). Later, as the title character in *Stavisky* (1974), directed by the masterful hand of Alain Resnais, Belmondo is absolutely marvelous as the pathological high-flying swindler, but the public at large preferred him in the more commercial films of De Broca and Verneuil (*Le Magnifique* (*The Magnificent One*, 1973, *Peur sur la ville* (*Fear Over the City*, 1974) and many other similar movies that were shot

Léaud in Godard's *Masculine / Feminine* (Godard, 1966).
Produced by Anatole Dauman

within the heart of the commercial French industry and far from the spirit of the New Wave).

Antoine Doinel and his descendants

The unbalanced, disjointed acting style brought by the New Wave has never been better illustrated than in the gestures, embarrassed smiles, and fake laughs of Jean-Pierre Léaud, an actor who may never have attracted unanimous praise, but who nonetheless could prove to be deeply moving because of his vulnerability. For *The 400 Blows*, Truffaut forbade him to smile, so that audiences would not pity him too much, as they had the child in *Dogs Without Collars* (1955). Léaud is also remarkable in his clumsy adolescence in *Antoine and Colette* (1962) and *Stolen Kisses* (1968). Godard seized upon these traits, fully exploiting them in *Masculine-Feminine* and *La Chinoise*.

117

Only Léaud fully incarnates the discomfort of pre-1968 young French men, allowing him to create very realistic relations with the young women, played by Chantal Goya, Anne Wiazemski, and Juliet Berto in particular, who were, for him at least, always unattainable or incomprehensible. Along the same line, Jean Eustache featured him in *Santa Claus Has Blue Eyes*, and later, of course, he was the disillusioned, smooth-talking dandy of *The Mother and the Whore*, caught between Bernadette Lafont and the amazing Françoise Lebrun. That long feature, lasting 3 hours and 40 minutes, is the quintessential post-New Wave movie; it remains authentic in its faithfulness to the New Wave's initial principles, a film that François Truffaut never dared to write, much less direct.

The New Wave also promoted a certain sort of actor who was directed in a more Jansenist manner along the models set by Jacques Becker's sober movie, *Le Trou* (*The Hole*, 1960) and the "inexpressivity" of Robert Bresson, whose *Pickpocket* (1959) had an underlying influence on all of the new French cinema of the time. Actors belonging to this tendency include Michel Subor from *Le Petit Soldat*, Charles Aznavour in *Shoot the Piano Player*, as well as Marc Michel who deliberately "underplays" in *Lola* (1961) and Claude Mann in *Bay of Angels* (1962), both directed by Jacques Demy. Jean-Pierre Melville also explored this path in *Léon Morin*, *Priest* and *Le Doulos* (*The Fingerman*, 1963) by suppressing the extraverted narcissism of his actors. Alain Robbe-Grillet directed Jacques Doniol-Valcroze in *L'Immortelle* and Jean-Louis Trintignant in *L'Homme qui ment* (*The Man Who Lies*, 1969) along the same lines.

Amateur actors, anonymous bodies

Some major New Wave films took their rejection of professionalism to the extreme by engaging only amateur actors, many of whom then remained relatively unknown. This was a process followed by Robert Bresson. Exemplary in this group of actors is Nadine Ballot, the young high-school girl followed by Jean Rouch's camera in *La Pyramide humaine* (*The Human Pyramid*, 1960) and *La Punition* (*The Punishment*, 1962), and who, in Rouch's short film *Gare du Nord* from the *Six in Paris* compilation, turns in a performance that equals any by a professional actress.

Doniol-Valcroze acts in a stiff, repressed style for *L'Immortelle* (Robbe-Grillet, 1963).
Produced by Samy Halfon and Michel Fano

Similarly, the exceptional aesthetic triumph of *Adieu Philippine*, labeled "the first television film" by Godard, is based on the established complicity between Jacques Rozier, who was more of an organizer of the improvised fiction than its director, and his three collaborating actors, Jean-Claude Aimini, Stefania Sabatini, and Yveline Céry. For instance, after the three main characters meet, Michel, the young television station technician, drags the two young women to a café to have a drink. This sort of scene, so common in cinema, is completely renewed by the actors' speech, the juke box music that accompanies their dialogue, Michel's clumsiness, the subtle jokes (as when Michel tells the waiter, who is exasperated with their indecision, "Don't panic Loulou, it's a tango," and the girls laugh wildly), and most of all by Rozier's editing, which, thanks, to the setting and rhythm, captures the spontaneity of everyday experience. As critic Jean-Louis Bory wrote in *Arts*: "Young, true, new, free, funny. A breath of fresh air. A glass of cool water. A day in the sun. Resnais, Truffaut, Godard, and the ghost

Michel (Aimini) jokes in the café; the two young women (Sabatini and Céry) are amused by his rambling flirtations in *Adieu Philippine* (Rozier, 1962).

Produced by Rome Paris Films, Unitec-Alpha, and Euro International Films

of Jean Vigo are protectively leaning over the cradle of *Adieu Philippine*. These godfathers are very good. But, Rozier does not need them. For a godmother, he has youth."[11]

Female Figures of the New Wave

Bernadette Lafont

Truffaut discovered this young woman from the southern French town of Nîmes for his short, *The Mischief Makers*, and she became the first real model of a New Wave woman, especially since she appears immediately afterward in films by Chabrol (*Le Beau Serge, Leda, The Good Girls*, and *Les Godelureaux*), as well as in Doniol-Valcroze's *A Game for Six Lovers*. Both these auteurs took full advantage of Lafont's natural sensuality, her stunning smile, and her liveliness. She was the closest to a Renoir-inspired actress that the New Wave would generate, springing from the influence of Catherine Rouvel and *Déjeuner sur l'herbe* (*Picnic on the Grass*, 1959). However, Chabrol and Doniol-Valcroze both restricted Lafont a bit too much to expressing a somewhat vulgar sensuality, especially in *The Good Girls*, where she constantly chews gum, and in *A Game for Six Lovers*, where she parades around in her underwear for much of the film. Later, Truffaut offered a tribute to her exuberance and love of life by giving her the terrific role in *Une belle fille comme moi* (*Such a Gorgeous Kid Like Me*, 1972), where she humiliates the young sociologist, played by André Dussolier, who interviews her in prison. Nelly Kaplan also celebrates her in *La Fiancée du pirate* (*The Pirate's Fiancée*, 1969). But it is Jean Eustache who presents her in a quite unexpected and remarkably convincing manner in *The Mother and the Whore*.

During the late 1950s, Bernadette Lafont thus offered a more modern image of the young southern French woman who is comfortable with her full figure, as well as natural, spontaneous, and populist; she was a tanned, brunette version of the blonde Juliette of St Tropez, played by Bardot in *And God Created Woman*, who had seemed far closer to an upper-class Parisian than a working-class southern French girl.

Lafont in *The Good Girls* (Chabrol, 1960).
Produced by Paris Film Productions and Panitalia

Karina and Godard: the "Dietrich–von Sternberg" of the New Wave

Even if Anna Karina performed as a comical character in Michel Deville's *Ce soir ou jamais* (*Tonight or Never*, 1961), her first real role on the screen was in *Le Petit Soldat*, which remained unreleased for three years after it had been banned by the censors. Her name remains irrevocably tied to Jean-Luc Godard, since he discovered her in 1960, married her, and offered her lead roles in seven feature films: *Le Petit Soldat, A Woman is a Woman, My Life to Live, Band of Outsiders, Pierrot le fou, Alphaville,* and *Made in USA*. Godard thereby returned to a certain Hollywood tradition, a close partnership between director and actress. They renewed the model established between Mack Sennett and Mabel Normand, Charlie Chaplin and Paulette Godard, and the unequaled example represented by Josef von Sternberg and Marlene Dietrich, from *The Blue Angel* (1930) to *The Devil is a Woman* (1935). In *Le Petit Soldat*, on his way to meet Karina's character Veronica, Bruno Forestier accompanies a friend who has made a bet that if he falls in

Karina in Deville's *Tonight or Never* (Deville, 1960).
Produced by Philippe Dussart

love with her, Bruno will have to pay him $50. Once she leaves, Bruno hands his friend a $50 bill without saying a word. In the same film there is a famous scene where Karina, as Veronica, poses for a long photo session in which the reporter frantically shoots her, taking shot after shot in what ends up being a magnificent declaration of love from the director to his actress. Similarly, in *My Life to Live*, Godard sets up a tragic, romantic tone near the end when he reads, in a voice-over using his own voice, the text of Edgar Allan Poe's *The Oval Portrait* to her character.

This biographical and passionate liaison is particularly rich for their shared work, since the tone and style common to these films follow the development of the couple's relations. *A Woman is a Woman* offers a moment of pure euphoria, an exuberant fantasy. Godard fully exploits Karina's Danish accent and even her comically unprofessional singing voice. He also takes advantage of her style of dress, which was based on three primary colors, as blue, white, and red irradiate from Angela's undergarments, playing falsely on her feigned "blue-stocking" traits. Next, she becomes a pathetic figure in the black-and-white *My Life to Live*, paralleling the Joan of Arc in Dreyer's silent movie; like Joan, her character here dies a tragic but also absurd death. But Karina's character rediscovers a sad yet playful gaiety in *Band of Outsiders* where she is as juvenile and moving as Raymond Queneau's Odile, for whom her character is named. In *Alphaville*, she is the unreal and robotic Natasha, daughter of Professor von Braun; Lemmy Caution helps her rediscover the meaning of words like "love" and "tenderness" by reading citations from Paul Eluard's *Capital of Pain*. But it is Marianne, Pierrot-Ferdinand's beloved in *Pierrot le fou*, that immortalized her for a whole generation of *cinéphiles*.

With *Made in USA*, Godard covers Karina with a Humphrey Bogart-style raincoat and loses his actress, like her character, in the meanderings of a plot that is as obscure as it is bloody and ornate. This was their final collaboration, but their partnership had been so close that all the other features directed by Godard during this era that did *not* involve Anna Karina in the lead role were marked by her absence. Even the blonde Camille of *Contempt*, played by Bardot, the biggest star of the era, transforms herself into a brunette in the middle of the movie to conjure up an echo of the director's absent wife.

Just as markedly as Jean-Pierre Léaud, in her own style, Anna Karina allowed the most prolific auteur of the New Wave to enrich the dramatic range of his female characters, thanks to her sense of fantasy and spontaneity. Following Jean Seberg, Karina helped continue the seductive attraction of actresses speaking the French language with a foreign accent, reviving the tradition springing from René Clair (Pola Illery in *Sous les toits de Paris* (*Under the Roofs of Paris*), 1930, a film referred to with the *Bastille Day* scene in *A Woman is a Woman*) and Jean Renoir (who used the incandescent Winna Winfried in *La Nuit du carrefour* (*Night at the Crossroad*), 1932), which is a reference point for *Made in USA*.

Jeanne and her sisters

If, to a certain degree, the Godard of the 1960s is the man with one woman, his colleague François Truffaut clearly fitted the title of his eventual movie,

The Man Who Loved Women, and only loved them in the plural sense. In the beginning was the mother, Claire Maurier, of *The 400 Blows*. Very quickly, and in very classical fashion, the feminine figures in Truffaut split into two sorts: the wife and the mistress. Nicole Berger and Marie Dubois set the pattern in *Shoot the Piano Player*, and, in more schizophrenic fashion and certainly with more tragedy and sadness, we have Françoise Dorléac in *Soft Skin*, and Catherine Deneuve, the tart, impersonating a wife and serving as a sexually passionate mistress in *The Siren of Mississippi*. The fragile Kiki Markham and Stacey Tendeter will provided more youthful renderings of these two emblematic faces.

The young girl resembles Marie-France Pisier and Claude Jade, the young woman who will marry Antoine Doinel. It is this variety, near bursting point, that is admirably displayed in *The Man Who Loved Women*, but it is for *Jules and Jim*'s Catherine, Truffaut's richest and more polymorphous character, that Jeanne Moreau assembles all of Truffaut's feminine figures: wife and mistress, she will alternately resemble Lena, Therese, Colette, Nicole, Linda, and Clarisse, Julie Kohler, Christine, and Marion. They are all nothing more than the different facets of the heroine Catherine, from *Jules and Jim*.

Finally, it is important to cite a number of young actresses whose glory was brief, lasting the duration of a movie or two, who nonetheless proved to be significant faces of the New Wave to the young audiences of the time. In personal letters from the era, published later, Godard claimed to have filmed *Breathless* for Anne Colette, who passed across the screens like a falling star following *All the Boys are Called Patrick*. The magazines for young *cinéphiles* gave a bit of attention to Juliette Mayniel, a "star" who quickly disappeared, but not before her large clear eyes had illuminated *The Cousins*, *Eyes Without a Face* (1960), for which Georges Franju wrapped her face in bandages, and *A Couple* by Jean-Pierre Mocky. Then she returned to Chabrol for *Ophélia* and *Landru* (both 1962), which proved fatal for her acting career.

For quite a while, Chabrol's filmography was tied to his second wife, Stéphane Audran, who first appeared in a minor role in *The Cousins* before moving into the foreground for *Les Bonnes Femmes*. But her career really took off later, after *Les Biches*, for what became the second creative phase of Chabrol's oeuvre, after he crossed the desert of the "Tiger" films. Nonetheless, Stéphane Audran's acting style, and the sort of roles she played in Chabrol's somber bourgeois melodramas and crime films such as *La Femme infidèle* (*The Unfaithful Wife*, 1969) and *Le Boucher* (*The Butcher*, 1970), were rather far removed from most New Wave actresses' performances.

As for the actresses discovered by Alain Resnais, such as Emmanuelle Riva and Delphine Seyrig, they came from the literary and dramatic worlds, benefiting from formative theatrical backgrounds. Thus, their styles too were quite different from the spontaneity and improvisation that characterized the New Wave. They stand in clear opposition to the young "non-professional" actresses employed by Jacques Rozier, or to Nadine Ballot of Rouch's fiction films.

Chapter Six
The New Wave's International Influence and Legacy Today

A S WE HAVE SEEN, the New Wave's appearance in France at the end of the 1950s marked a rejuvenation, bringing a new generation into the film industry at a time of creative sclerosis. It arrived 10–15 years after the Liberation, an interval that is both characteristic and original in the evolution of French society's cultural production. The sort of post-World War II disruption brought on by the Italian neorealist model of 1944–6 never occurred in France. The only emblematic film of the French resistance was *La Bataille du rail* (*Battle of the Rail*), directed in 1946 by René Clément, about the resistance of railroad workers, but Clément's ultimate career would be very different from that of his Italian counterparts such as Roberto Rossellini or Vittorio De Sica. Moreover, French directors like Clément, Becker, Bresson, and Clouzot remained strong individualists, isolated from one another, never coalescing into a collective cultural movement like the mythical neorealists of the same period just over the border in Italy.

The milieu of French intellectuals was thus much further removed from the film industry than was the case in Italy. Even when a philosopher as prestigious as Jean-Paul Sartre collaborated on scripts or dialogue for films like *Les Jeux sont faits* (*The Chips are Down*, 1947) by Jean Delannoy, or *Les Orgueilleux* (*The Proud Ones*, 1953) by Yves Allégret, the results were not always definitive or aesthetically productive.

An important area of inquiry posed by cinema history concerns the period just before the French New Wave and its relations to other "young cinemas" that appeared throughout the world at the turning point between the 1950s and 1960s. A certain French chauvinism sees its own cinema at the root of this international revolution. A closer analysis of the chronologies involved allows us to distinguish several movements of renewal and rupture prior to the French New Wave from those new aesthetic trends motivated more directly by the diffusion of the first feature films by Truffaut, Resnais, and Godard; Chabrol's features did not attract quite the same audience abroad.

Precursors

The disasters resulting from the global conflict of World War II do not seem to have had any direct repercussions in the realm of European film aesthetics, except in the case of the Italian neorealists. Certainly, from an industrial point of view, the war led to the disappearance of German cinema for a time and the quantitative reduction of Soviet productions.

Later, in his famous summary of film production for the years 1957–8 (cited in chapter 1), Pierre Billard called attention to the appearance of a number of new and original auteurs in the United States, the Soviet Union, Poland, Italy, and even Franco's repressive Spain. He cited Robert Aldrich, Grigori Tchoukhrai, Andrei Wajda, Francesco Maselli, and Juan Antonio Bardem. By contrast, France seemed to offer only Roger Vadim and Michel Boisrond.

If we widen the inquiry, we can argue that the 1950s were marked, on both the cultural and political levels, by the hegemony of Hollywood, the crisis of Stalinism, and the difficulties of decolonization, which brought on a new round of concerns regarding the ethics and moral values within most major film-producing nations.[1] Yet this decade also witnessed a crisis within the dominant American film studios. Despite their economic domination of the world markets, Hollywood studios were burdened with changing conditions of domestic production, expensive super-productions, and the emergence of independent producers such as Robert Aldrich and Richard Brooks. Meanwhile, the state-run national cinemas, like those in Eastern Europe, tried to escape the dogmas of "Socialist Realism," imposed some-

128

what in vain by Jdanov and the Soviet Union. Italian neorealism did not directly influence these new auteurs. It was the Polish cinema that provided the first example of a certain aesthetic emancipation, with the cinema of Andrei Wajda. He began in 1954 with a movie that bore an emblematic title, *A Generation*. With *Canal* (1956) and *Ashes and Diamonds* (1958), he definitively distanced himself from the codes of Socialist Realism, just like his contemporary colleague Andrei Munk, whose *Eroica* (*Heroism*, 1957) and *Bad Luck* (1960) harbored a very ironic tone and avoided using the standard epic heroism.

In Sweden, Ingmar Bergman pursued a solitary path, creating an oeuvre more and more isolated from the models that dominated conventional scripts. He began in 1945 with *Crisis*, but it was only after his tenth feature film that he developed his auteur output, becoming more and more distinctive. This style was revealed in a stunning manner with *Summer with Monika* (1953), a film that greatly impressed the young critics François Truffaut and Jean-Luc Godard with its liberated tone and the frank presentation of the romantic relations between its two Swedish adolescents.

In Spain, Franco's state-run production schedule, dominated by popular comedies and conventional melodramas, nevertheless allowed a bit of room for several neorealist-like projects that were fairly original to Europe. These included Juan Antonio Bardem's first two features *Death of a Cyclist* (1955) and *Main Street* (1956), both produced by Georges de Beauregard. But both these films were far from the New Wave aesthetic.

The years 1959–60 were characterized by the appearance of a number of new directors, spread around the globe, who broke with the aesthetic norms of their times. Their disruptions often paralleled those undertaken by the New Wave, without necessarily having any direct influence. In most cases, one or two directors completed an original first feature. These assorted films premiered in theaters at about the same time as Truffaut's and Rivette's first features were being distributed around the globe. This coincidence encouraged in a radical way the steps begun by foreign auteurs, who, following the example of these initial French triumphs, struggled to continue their fledgling careers despite the hurdles offered by their various national industries. According to the findings of historian Barthélemy Amengual, a similar process characterizes the initiation and progress of several new waves, even in the socialist nations during the 1950s. Such conditions, exemplary in the case of French cinema, could be found to certain degrees all over:

> To begin with, critics orchestrated a conflict between the old and younger generations in the areas of aesthetics, ideology, and even morality. One or two magazines ventured to support those champions of change who typically entered the profession by the backdoor: independent productions with low budgets, reduced technical crews, beginning actors. For everyone, Italian neorealism offered the strongest model (even though it was banned in Eastern Bloc countries), but they also looked to the example and experience provided by documentary practice. The new films circulated. Praise echoed back from foreign shores. The media got involved. A new public, prepared by ciné-clubs, cinémathèques, film festivals, art house circuits, and specialized magazines, proved ready. Film schools and institutes fired up. The officials in charge of the cinema, and even producers, allowed themselves to be convinced. The wave is launched. Several years of excitement, comprehension, and occasionally real successes followed, and then it would all dissolve away or become integrated [into the mainstream national cinema].[2]

The situation in Great Britain, however, corresponded only partially to this model. The so-called "Angry Young Men" movement first intervened in the fields of literature and theater, and was more open to avant-garde practice. It was from this path of adapting provocative plays that young directors launched the Free Cinema movement, with films like *Room at the Top* (Jack Clayton, 1958), which was adapted from John Braine's 1957 novel, or, especially, *Look Back in Anger* (1959), which Tony Richardson adapted from a play by John Osborne. These were followed by the films of Karel Reisz (*Saturday Night and Sunday Morning*, 1960), a director who came from British documentary, and Lindsay Anderson (*This Sporting Life*, 1963), who had founded the journal *Sequence* in 1946. The latter was a film critic for *The Times* and *Observer*, and author of a manifesto entitled "Stand Up! Stand Up!," published in *Sight and Sound*, which was every bit as virulent as François Truffaut's "A Certain Tendency of the French Cinema."

Even in the United States, but far from the Hollywood studios, the experimental cinema and documentary movement were influenced by the appearance of new practices. In New York, a new style of reportage grew up around Robert Drew, leading to the birth of direct cinema via the films of Drew (*Yankee No*, and *Primary*, 1960), as well as Albert and David Maysles, and Donn Pennebaker. The young actor John Cassavetes was inspired by musical improvisation, springing from avant-garde jazz, notably Charles Mingus, in directing his first 16mm version of *Shadows* in 1957, followed by a second version in 1959. This movie is just as original as *Breathless* in terms of its direction of the actors, improvised dialogue, and editing rhythms. However, it remained largely unknown by French critics, who would only discover the significance of Cassavetes when his *Husbands* opened ten years later in 1970.

In Japan, Nagisha Oshima started out as assistant, then wrote reviews and scripts before directing his first three consecutive, very personal features: *A Town of Love and Hope* (1959), *Cruel Story of Youth* (1960), and *Burial of the Sun* (1960). Immediately afterward he proved himself leader of the "Japanese New Wave" with *Night and Fog in Japan* (1960), his tribute to Alain Resnais. The political audacity of his work, in which Oshima violently denounced the renewal of the Japanese–American Treaty, caused quite a scandal in his nation. Working in parallel with his directing, Oshima continued to write analytical reviews for film journals, especially of French New Wave movies, such as *Breathless*, which he greatly admired.

The Influence of the New Wave on International Cinema

The discovery of the new French films provoked strong reactions in the State-run cinema schools of Eastern Europe. Poland was first to act and was quickly imitated by young directors in Czechoslovakia and Hungary. In Poland, the young poet Jerzy Skolimowski, who had worked as a scriptwriter for Wajda's *Innocent Sorcerers* (1960) and Roman Polanski's *Knife in the Water* (1962), went on to direct *Identification Marks: None* in 1964, for which he was the writer, art director, editor, and principal actor. The movie is intensely subjective, written as an essay, and would have been unthinkable without Godard having first pointed the way by overturning cinematic forms. Skolimowski continued with *Walkover* (1965) and *Barrier* (1966) before leaving Poland in 1967 after his outrageous satire, *Hands Up!*, was banned by the censors. That same year he made his most Godardian film yet, *Departure*, starring Jean-Pierre Léaud as a young hairdresser fascinated by automobile racing.

As for Czechoslovakia, there was first a timid liberalization around 1956 when several films by Jan Kadar and Vojtech Jasny appeared, but it was really after 1963 that a new generation just out of the state-run film school, FAMU, revealed its existence on the world's screens with several stunning films full of youth and spontaneity. Most important were Milos Forman's *Black Peter* (1963) and *Loves of a Blonde* (1965), Jaromil Jires's *The First Cry*, and Vera Chytilova's *Something Different*, both from 1963. Other young directors followed, including Ewald Schorm, Jan Nemec, Ivan Passer, and Jiri Menzel, among others. They were so numerous that one now speaks of the "Prague School." As students in their classes at FAMU, they had all watched Truffaut's *The 400 Blows* and Godard's *Breathless* over and over.

On the other side of the globe, it was the Brazilian cinema that launched a "cinema novo," in response to the New Wave and especially Godard. As in many other places throughout the world, Brazil possessed a new generation that was a product of ciné-clubs and student movements who grabbed hold of cameras hoping to produce films marked by the decolonialization of cultural forms. A dozen such new auteurs sprang up around Ruy Guerra, Carlos Diegues, and Joaquim Pedro de Andrade. But the most brilliant of them was clearly Glauber Rocha who, following his rather hybrid production, *The Turning Wind* (1962), presented a flamboyant, even baroque political trilogy – *Black God, White Devil, Land in Anguish*, and *Antonio das Mortes* – that would prove important for cinema history in 1964–69. Glauber Rocha became the spokesperson for this "cinema novo," as well as a formidable polemicist, exploiting his pen as casually and provocatively as the images he created on the screen. In 1963 he published *A Critical Revision of Brazilian Cinema*. But we must not forget Nelson Pereira Dos Santos, who preceded the "cinema novo" with his *Rio, 40 Degrees* (1956) and *Rio, North Zone* (1957), both of which greatly influenced Rocha. Moreover, he edited *The Turning Wind*. His *Barren Lives* (1960) was also very important for young directors, and he himself had been very influenced by the Italian neorealists, especially Rossellini and De Santis.

Italy's situation was fairly unusual. It had gone through its cinematic "revolution" with the fall of fascism, beginning in 1943–4 with films such as *Ossessione* and *Rome, Open City*. The postwar years were very rich, and the decade of the 1950s saw development of major works by a number of auteurs, including Luchino Visconti, who was influenced by opera and the theater, Federico Fellini, who looked to comic strips and humorous caricature, and Michelangelo Antonioni, who was fascinated with documentary practice. But the years 1959–60 witnessed more radical changes in aesthetic practice. Following *The Cry* (1957), Antonioni created a new narrative rhythm based on de-dramatization and elliptical storytelling with *L'Avventura* (1959). Fellini threw himself into his protean work with *La Dolce Vita* (1960), and Visconti ventured forth with a revised neorealism, thanks to the Verga-inspired realism / naturalism of *Rocco and His Brothers* (1960). The Italian cinema was thus much less ossified than its French counterpart had been in 1956–7.

However, the very personal form seen in Roberto Rossellini's early 1950s filmic narratives, especially those inspired by his relationship with Ingrid Bergman – *Stromboli* (1950), *Europa 51* (1952), and *Voyage to Italy* (1953) – were misunderstood and underappreciated by Italian critics of this era, who were still attached to a notion of pure neorealism as seen in Rossellini's *Paisan*. It was actually French criticism, begun with the famous essay by Jacques Rivette in *Cahiers du Cinéma*, that helped safeguard Rossellini's significance:

> It seems impossible to me that anyone can look at *Voyage to Italy* without recognizing right away that this film opens a passageway that all cinema should follow to avoid certain death; . . . but here is what I saw: Rossellini's movies, although staged, also obey this aesthetic of direct cinema, with all the advantages that entails, with all its impossible risks, tension, chance, and providence.[3]

It was also at this moment that a director like Francesco Rosi could completely renew the political intrigue movie with his brilliant *Salvatore Giulano* (1961), constructed as a puzzle with flashbacks and fragments of hypothetical biographies. In a certain sense, the modern Italian cinema did not wait for the lessons provided by the New Wave before creating its own major works of European cinema, such as Antonioni's trilogy, *L'Avventura*, *La Notte*, and *Eclipse*, Visconti's *Leopard*, or Fellini's *8½*.

All the same, the effects of the French New Wave are observable in the first efforts by young directors like Bernardo Bertolucci (*Before the Revolution*, 1967, and then the very Godardian *Partner*, 1968), or Marco Bellocchio (*Fists in the Pockets*, 1965). They can also be spotted in the first cinematic projects by the young poet Pier Paolo Pasolini, whose work transformed the codes of neorealism beginning with *Accatone* (1961) and *Momma Roma* (1962), by accentuating research on plasticity and forms, inspired by Brecht. Pasolini went on to develop a critical and creative dialogue with Godard throughout the 1960s, beginning with *RoGoPaG* (1963), where they collaborated on the episodic project, up until *Pigsty* (1970). Just like Rocha during this era, Pasolini even borrowed specific actors from the French New Wave, such as using Jean-Pierre Léaud (in *Pigsty*, as well as Rocha's *The Lion Has Seven Heads*, 1969), and Pierre Clementi (*Pigsty*, but also Bertolucci's *Partner* and *Conformist*, 1970, and Rocha's *Heads Cut Off*, 1970).

By 1969–70, the modern cinema transcended national boundaries, while aesthetic interactions became the rule with creative forces such as Godard, Pasolini, and Glauber Rocha, but also Ingmar Bergman, Luis Buñuel, and Federico Fellini, all of whom directed their films in a freer fashion, clear of all rigorous narrative constraints. This was all a consequence of the international reception of French films of the New Wave that had begun in 1960.

We have referred to the new documentary forms appearing in the American investigative cinema around 1959 and 1960, especially with Robert Drew and Richard Leacock. This movement intervened in an even more spectacular manner with the New Wave when French Canadian cinema began to make regular exchanges between Jean Rouch's camera operators and the National Film Board. The central figure in this interaction was Michel Brault. He backed up the poet Pierre Perrault when he began *Pour la suite du monde* (*For Those Who Will Follow*) in 1963. But the new Québécois cinema was not limited to documentary practice. A number of young directors began to discover their own country thanks to a most original and personal form of cinematic expression. The auteur who demonstrated the most marked influence of the Jean-Luc Godard of *Les Carabiniers* was surely Jean-Pierre Lefebvre, originally a critic for the journal *Objectif*, then director of *Révolutionnaire* (1965), a first feature film that is a political essay with a very free style. It would be followed by many other films, but Lefebvre was certainly not the only participant; from 1965 on, a new expressive francophone cinema would receive international distribution, including the films of Gilles Carle, Gilles Groult, Claude Jutra, and Denys Arcand.

The New Wave, Avant-Garde, and Experimental Cinema

At various points in its existence, the French cinema has witnessed periods rich in experimental research, as, for instance, during the period beginning in 1917, with the arrival of the first feature films by Abel Gance (*La Roue* (*The Wheel*), 1922), Marcel L'Herbier (*L'Inhumaine* (*New Enchantment*), 1924), and Jean Epstein (*Coeur fidèle* (*Faithful Heart*), 1923), then a bit later, the surrealist films by Buñuel and Dali (*Un chien andalou* (*An Andalusian Dog*), 1928, and *L'Age d'or* (*The Age of Gold*), 1930) and Jean Cocteau's contributions (*Le Sang d'un poète* (*Blood of the Poet*), 1930). During the 1950s, this tendency is made concrete in the "lettriste" cinema of Isidore Isou and Maurice Lemaitre.

Paradoxically, the New Wave's movies would push the vague subversive desires of these creative young directors into feature-length narrative filmmaking. The truly "experimental" cinema – that is, the non-narrative and sometimes non-representational form – would disappear for a few years, only to return in the mid-1960s with the first films by Philippe Garrel (*Les Enfants désaccordés* (*Out of Tune Children*) in 1964, *Anémone*, and *Marie pour mémoire* (*Marie for Memory*) both in 1967) as well as Marcel Hanoun (*Octobre à Madrid* (*October in Madrid*), 1965, and *L'Eté* (*Summer*), 1968), and Jean-Pierre Lajournade (*Le Jouer de quilles* (*The Skittle Player*), 1968, and *La Fin des Pyrénées* (*The End of the Pyrenees*), 1971). Nonetheless, Jean-Daniel Pollet, director of the first New Wave film never to find a distributor, the mythical *La Ligne de mire* (*The Focal Line*, 1960), would provide one of the masterpieces of the avant-garde cinema in 1963, *La Méditerranée* (*The Mediterranean*), with its voice-over commentary spoken by Philippe Sollers. Several years after 1968, this experimental tendency would enrich a number of works, but not without causing friction with the political cinema, which was only rarely preoccupied with questions of cinematic écriture.

The Historical Consequences of the Movement: The New Wave Today

One of the New Wave's most direct consequences was to impose the idea that cinematic creation requires a regular renewal by young directors. Mechanisms put in place within France during the 1970s have promoted the continued flowering of first features, though few of them are very promising. An advance on box office receipts is now reserved for the production of first films that can be financed on the presentation of a scenario. Roughly 30 films are produced each year under these circumstances, which represents, on average, about one quarter of all French films. It has become almost as easy to produce a first feature as to publish a first novel, even though the financial investment necessary is nowhere near comparable. But out of the hundreds of new directors, very few authentic new auteurs appear.

What is striking is the continued absence of a collective movement. The example set by all the former *Cahiers* critics who have followed in the steps of the first generation – Truffaut, Godard, Chabrol, Rivette, and Rohmer – provides a telling test case. While, successively, Luc Moullet, André Téchiné, Pascal Kané, Jean-Louis Comalli, Serge Le Peron, Danièle Dubroux, Léos Carax, and Olivier Assayas all wrote for *Cahiers* and then made movies, they in no way present a coherent group like that of the 1958 generation. However, Paul Vecchiali has tried, by the intermediary of a production company, Les Films Diagonale, to stimulate a team of young auteurs connected by shared interests: Jean-Claude Guiguet, Marie-Claude Treilhou, Jean-Claude Biette, Jacques Davila, and Gérard Frot-Coutaz. But the venture has remained somewhat marginal, since the box office returns and international distribution for their films have remained fairly modest.

Only André Téchiné, after a difficult beginning, has successfully attained a spot in cinematic production roughly equivalent to that held by François Truffaut prior to Truffaut's death in 1984. Téchiné owes his triumph to the unfailing support he receives from the internationally famous star Catherine Deneuve, beginning with his *Hôtel des Amériques* (*Hotel of the*

Americas, 1981) through *Ma saison préférée* (*My Favorite Season*, 1993), to *Les Voleurs* (*Thieves*, 1996).

But if the younger auteurs found it difficult to thrive within French cinema during the 1980s and 1990s, a period dominated by the strong presence of Maurice Pialat (whose *Van Gogh* was one of the rare masterpieces of 1990s French cinema), it was in part because they had to compete with the now aging New Wave filmmakers, who remained as inventive as they had always been. Truffaut died in 1984 leaving a legacy of 21 features, while Pierre Kast and Jacques Doniol-Valcroze died in 1989 and Jacques Demy in 1990. By contrast, Jean-Luc Godard passed the 40-feature mark with his *Forever Mozart* (1996), not counting the many short films and hours of television production he has accomplished. In 2001, his *Eloge à l'amour* (*In Praise of Love*) was a great critical success at Cannes and beyond as well. In 1997, Chabrol completed his 50th feature film with *Rien ne va plus* (*Swindle*); he has made more than 20 films for television, and in 2001 he shows no sign of slowing down. Despite initial problems getting their careers started, Jacques Rivette and Eric Rohmer continue to produce important films: Rivette has provided more than 15 features (with some, such as *Out One* and *Belle Noiseuse* being very long works), while Rohmer has made more than 20. Rohmer's creative originality is indeed astounding, since his more recent "Comedies and Proverbs" and "Moral Tales" often seem even more liberated and youthful than his earliest movies. At the age of 80, he remains more than ever the director of adolescence and young people of today.

This high output among the original New Wave directors is only a partial explanation As we saw in the first chapter, directors like André Berthomieu and Jean Boyer possess filmographies that are just as lengthy. Rather, an historical chance allowed a modest ciné-club in the Latin Quarter and a small film journal to bring together a dozen auteurs united by discovery and love for the cinema. At any other moment in history, they might have been moved instead into writing novels, undertaking anthropology, journalism, art history, literary theory, or launching some enterprise.

Raymond Borde, after having initially opposed the *Cahiers du Cinéma* team when he was a critic writing alongside his friends at *Positif*, returned to the theses of his attacks of 1962 for the preface to Francis Courtade's polemical book on the many curses and problems facing French cinema, *Les Malédictions du cinéma français*:

> For this stage of analysis, I think I must introduce the topic of the ultimate factor of pure chance, people. I really understood the *Positif* of the late 1950s. We were exemplary moralists, we were not filmmakers. Some among us, such as Bernard Chardère, Louis Seguin, Jacques Demeure from television, and Ado Kyrou, for instance, had handled a camera and directed quite rigorous short films, but none of us was a "cinema fanatic." We lacked the sort of motivation that has already enabled Chabrol to complete his 37th feature (in 1977). Thus we were – and here I refer to our collective document, which was often quite lucid, entitled *La Nouvelle Vague* and published in *Premier Plan* – obliged to bet on paltry values. To the detestable and sanctimonious right wing *Cahiers* critics (this is still Borde writing), we can only counter with Georges Franju (who has already said what is most important), Claude-Bernard Aubert, Paul Paviot, Robert Menegoz, Jean-Claude Bonnardot, Louis Grospierre, and Pierre Kast. . . . It was touching. What a riot.[4]

Indeed.

The Perpetuity of the New Wave Films

Finally, it is essential to consider one last criterion, which involves the power and originality of the central films directed by French filmmakers in the years bridging the 1950s and 1960s. When projected today, roughly 40 years later, *The 400 Blows, Hiroshima mon amour, The Cousins, Breathless*, but also *Me, a Black Man, Paris Belongs to Us, Adieu Philippine, Lola, Cléo de 5 à 7*, not to mention *Pierrot le fou* and even as marginal a short film as Rohmer's *The Girl at the Monceau Bakery* (and we could easily extend the list to more than 30 titles), are all just as lively as when they first appeared, because they miraculously knew how to seize the most authentic "present tense" of their era. When discovered today at the beginning of a new century by French film students born in the 1980s, these films can still generate an emotional effect that is just as remarkable as the results provoked in the young viewers of 1960.

The same holds for international filmgoers who are still, and again, discovering French society and its behavior, lifestyles, gestures, ways of speaking, moral attitudes, etc., via the films of François Truffaut, Jean-Luc Godard, and Eric Rohmer. This is equivalent to how the world's *cinéphiles* have come to know New York City or the various American landscapes from watching Hollywood's films, without ever setting foot in America. The New Wave audience worldwide today consists of both *cinéphiles* and college students. The latter are initiated into the history of cinema in part by watching Truffaut and Godard, and, as a result, the subsequent generations of American, Asian, and Middle Eastern filmmakers have learned much from *Shoot the Piano Player* and *Band of Outsiders*, as clearly seen in the movies of Martin Scorsese and Quentin Tarantino, among others, and of course Jean-Pierre Melville has proven to be a huge influence on Paul Schrader and John Woo.

It is obviously not just their discourse that makes these films retain their youth and vigor; it is certainly the way in which this discourse is delivered to the spectator. New Wave films appeared at the same moment that jazz was becoming more "free" and undergoing radical formal and stylistic upheavals. Similarly, the New Wave became a field for experimentation in cinematic creation that proved just as varied and rich as that of Soviet cinema in the 1920s. Godard provides the most obvious example, but even Rivette's explorations throughout the decade culminated in a unique film, *L'Amour fou* (*Mad Love*, 1968). The New Wave proved to be an aesthetic revolution that forever marked film history. In the strictest sense, the only true heirs to the New Wave of 1959 were Jean Eustache (from *Mauvaises Fréquentations* (*Bad Company*), 1963, to *Photos d'Alix* (*Photos of Alix*), 1981) and Philippe Garrel (from *Lit de la vierge* (*The Virgin's Bed*), 1969, to *Baisers de secours* (*Kisses of Help*), 1989, to *J'entends plus la guitare* (*I No Longer Hear the Guitar*), 1991, to *Coeur fantôme* (*Phantom Heart*), 1995), both of whom, in their own manner, have prolonged the experimental ventures of their predecessors.

It is even regrettable that the original New Wave films, so vibrant in themselves, have been co-opted by marketing and commodification as trinkets: images from the films are sold on everything from posters and t-shirts to ashtrays. But this is the inevitable price of success in the "society of spectacle." The best way to console ourselves is by going back to the movies, rediscovering the films themselves for the first or fiftieth time, in a film theater, like the first day of their public premiere.

"All in all, if you've got to . . . you've got to," as Michel Poiccard proclaims at the opening of *Breathless*.

Appendix
Chronology of Major Political and Cultural Events, 1956–63[1]

1956

Political/Cultural Events

- Khrushchev's meeting with the American Communist Party's 20th Congress, denouncing "the Cult of Personality"
- French decree calls upon all "eligible" young men for military service (for the Algerian conflict)
- the Suez Canal is nationalized by Egypt's President Nasser
- Soviet troops intervene in Budapest
- Break occurs between Jean-Paul Sartre and the French Communist Party

Films

Michel Strogoff (Gallone)
Hunchback of Notre Dame (Delannoy)
Gervaise (Clément)
A Man Escaped (Bresson)
Elena et les hommes (*Paris Does Strange Things*, Renoir)
The Picasso Mystery (Clouzot)
And God Created Woman (Vadim)
The Silent World (Malle-Cousteau)
Night and Fog (Resnais)
Four Bags Full (Autant-Lara)

1957

Political/Cultural Events
- first revelations about French use of torture in Algeria (*Le Monde* and *Témoinage chrétien*)
- creation of the "internationale situationniste"
- network of aid established in France for the FLN (by F. Jeanson)

Films
Le Triporteur (*The Tricyclist*, Pinoteau)
Porte des Lilas (*Gates of Paris*, Clair)
The Spies (Clouzot)
La Parisienne (Boisrond)
Assassins et voleurs (*Thieves and Assassins*, Guitry)
Elevator to the Gallows (Malle)
One Never Knows (Vadim)

1958

Political/Cultural Events
- European institutions are established in Brussels
- Henri Alleg publishes *La Question* on torture in Algeria and the "Maurice Audin Affair," about the professor kidnapped and killed by French soldiers; the book is banned
- a Committee of Friendship toward the people of Algeria is established and calls upon de Gaulle to step back into politics
- National Assembly nominates De Gaulle for president (June)
- Françoise Giroud publishes *The New Wave: Portrait of Youth*
- André Malraux is named minister in charge of "expanding the influence of French culture"

Films
Les Miserables (Le Chanois)
The Cheats (Carné)
L'Eau vive (*The Girl and the River*, Villiers)
En cas de malheur (*In Case of Adversity/Love is my Profession*, Autant-Lara)
Mon Oncle (Tati)
The Lovers (Malle)
Me, a Black Man (Rouch)
A Life (Astruc)
Montparnasse 19 (Becker)
The Mischief Makers (Truffaut)
Barrage Against the Pacific (Clément)
Goha (Barratier)
Back Against the Wall (Molinaro)

- French Fifth Republic is formed (September)
- Charles de Gaulle is elected in a universal, indirect vote (December)

1959

Political/Cultural Events
- Castro's revolution in Cuba
- F. Maspero creates his publishing house
- Edgar Morin writes his *Autocritique*, an intellectual account of experience with the French Communist Party, then he quits the party
- the journal *Esprit* publishes a special issue on leisure
- Louis Althusser writes *Montesquieu, Politics and History*
- first broadcast of "Salue les copains" on the radio

Films
La Vache et le prisonnier (*The Cow and the Prisoner*, Verneuil)
Pickpocket (Bresson)
Picnic on the Grass (Renoir)
La Tête contre les murs (*The Keepers*, Franju)
Dangerous Liaisons, 1960 (Vadim)
Black Orpheus (Camus)
Hiroshima mon amour (Resnais)
Le Beau Serge (Chabrol)
Zazie in the Metro (Malle)
The Cousins (Chabrol)
The 400 Blows (Truffaut)
Two Men in Manhattan (Melville)

1960

Political/Cultural Events
- death of Albert Camus
- first French atomic bomb successfully exploded
- Jeanson's Trial; the "Manifesto of 121," proclaiming it is morally correct to refuse to serve in the military, fighting the Algerian War, is distributed

Films
The Truth (Clouzot)
Le Passage du Rhin (*Passage on the Rhine*, Cayatte)
Moderato Cantabile (Brooks)
Une aussi longue absence (*Such a Long Absence*, Colpi)
Breathless (Godard)
The Good Girls (Chabrol)

- *Hara-Kiri* #1 is published
- counter-demonstration by French Algerian intellectuals (October)

Shoot the Piano Player (Truffaut)
The Hole (Becker)

1961

Political/Cultural Events

- referendum on self-determination in Algeria (winning 75% of the vote)
- first pamphlets by the OAS; attempted coup d'état in Algeria by Generals Challe, Salan, Jouhaud, and Zeller
- construction of Berlin Wall is begun
- *Partisans* #1 is published, beginning recognition and solidarity for the "Third World"
- Islamic demonstrations in Paris against the installation of curfews: 250 participants are killed
- the first of the government's Centers for Culture is established in Le Havre.

Films

Un taxi pour Tobrouk (*A Taxi to Tabrook*, De la Patellière)
Paris Belongs to Us (Rivette)
Last Year at Marienbad (Resnais)
You Won't Kill Again (Autant-Lara)
Leon Morin, Priest (Melville)
Lola (Demy)
A Woman is a Woman (Godard)
The Testament of Dr Cordelier (Renoir)
L'Enclos (*Enclosure*, Gatti)
La Morte saison des amours (*Season of Lover*, Kast)
Chronicle of a Summer (Rouch)

1962

Political/Cultural Events

- numerous attacks by the OAS
- anti-OAS demonstration in Paris: 8 dead at Charonne Métro station
- cease-fire in Algeria with the signing of the Evian Accords
- referendum: 90% favor the Evian Accords (April)
- Georges Pompidou becomes Prime Minister
- official recognition of an independent Algeria
- *Salue les copains* #1 is published; rocker Johnny Halliday is on the cover
- death of Marilyn Monroe
- assassination attempt on the life of de Gaulle by Petit-Clamart, organized by OAS
- Che Guevara goes to Moscow, beginning his mythical status
- Cuban missile crisis
- referendum on universal suffrage: 61% favor electing the French president by national vote

Films

La Guerre des boutons (*The War of Buttons*, Robert)

Le Repos de guerrier (*The Warrior's Rest*, Vadim)

Le Caporal épinglé (*The Elusive Corporal*, Renoir)

Private Life (Malle)

Procès de Jeanne d'Arc (*Trial of Joan of Arc*, Bresson)

My Life to Live (Godard)

Jules and Jim (Truffaut)

The Immortal One (Robbe-Grillet)

Sign of Leo (Rohmer)

Cléo from 5 to 7 (Varda)

Thérèse Desqueyroux (Franju)

Cuba, si (Marker)

1963

Political/Cultural Events

- Jean Vilar, disagreeing with the directors, refuses to return as director of the Theatre National de Paris
- Juan Grimau is executed on Franco's order
- Pope Jean XXIII dies; Paul VI is chosen
- relations between the Soviet Union and China are Moscow and Beijing are broken off
- death of Jean Cocteau
- President Kennedy is shot dead in Dallas
- *Lui* #1 appears
- center for radio is begun in Paris

Films

Mélodie en sous-sol (*The Big Snatch* (UK), *Any Number Can Win* (USA), Verneuil)

Les Tontons flingueurs (*Monsieur Gangster*, Lautner)

Le Soupirant (*The Suitor*, Etaix)

Le Feu follet (*The Fire Within*, Malle)

Muriel (Resnais)

Les Parapluies de Cherbourg (*Umbrellas of Cherbourg*, Demy)

Les Carabiniers (Godard)

Le Mépris (Godard)

Le Joli Mai (Marker)

La Jetée (Marker)

Mourir à Madrid (*To Die in Madrid*, Rossif)

Codine (Colpi)

Adieu Philippine (Rozier)

Notes

Introduction

1. Since the original publication of Marie's book, several new studies of the French New Wave have appeared, including Antoine de Baecque, *La Nouvelle Vague: portrait d'une jeunesse* (Paris: Flammarion, 1998), Jean Douchet, *French New Wave*, trans. Robert Bonnono (New York: Distributed Art Publishers, 1999), and Richard Neupert, *A History of the French New Wave* (Madison: University of Wisconsin Press, 2002).
2. Jean-Luc Douin, *La Nouvelle Vague 25 ans après* (Paris: Editions du CERF, 1983).
3. Anne Gillain, *Les Quatre Cents Coups de François Truffaut* (Paris: Nathan, 1991); Carole Le Berre, *François Truffaut* (Paris: Cahiers du Cinéma, 1993); Jean-Louis Leutrat, *Hiroshima mon amour d'Alain Resnais* (Paris: Nathan, 1994); Michel Cieutat, *Pierrot le fou* (Limonset: Editions L'Interdisciplinaire, 1993); Dudley Andrew, *Breathless* (New Brunswick: Rutgers University Press, 1987); Berthélemy Amengual, *Bande à part* (Crisnée, Belgium: Editions Yellow Now, 1993); and also see Michel Marie, *Le Mépris* (Paris: Nathan, 1995) and *A Bout de souffle* (Paris: Nathan, 1999).
4. René Prédal, *Cinquante ans de cinéma français* (Paris: Nathan, 1996).
5. Jacques Siclier, *Le Cinéma français: I. De La Bataille du Rail à La Chinoise, 1945–1968* and *II. De Baisers volés à Cyrano de Bergerac, 1968–1900* (Paris: Editions Ramsay Cinéma, 1990 and 1991); Jean-Michel Frodon, *L'Age moderne du cinéma français* (Paris: Flammarion, 1995).
6. Alan Williams, *Republic of Images* (Cambridge: Harvard University Press, 1992), Susan Hayward, *French National Cinema* (London: Routledge, 1993),

and Ginette Vincendeau, *The Companion to French Cinema* (London: BFI/Cassell, 1996).

Chapter 1 A Journalistic Slogan and a New Generation

1. "Le Rapport sur la jeunesse," *Express* (December 12, 1957): 15.
2. Françoise Audé, *Ciné-modèle, cinéma d'elles* (Paris: L'Age d'homme, 1981).
3. *France-Observateur* 501 (December 3, 1959).
4. Ibid.
5. For a detailed account of this colloquium, see Jean-Michel Frodon's *L'Age moderne du cinéma français* (Paris: Flammarion, 1995).
6. André-Sylvain Labarthe, *Essai sur le jeune cinéma français* (Paris: Terrain Vague, 1960).
7. Raymond Borde, Freddy Buache, and Jean Curtelin, *Nouvelle Vague* (Paris: Serdoc, 1962).
8. Ibid., p. 14.
9. For more information, see the chart in Jean-Pierre Jeancolas, *Le Cinéma des français* (Paris: Nathan, 1985), pp. 12–13.
10. Pierre Billard, "40 moins 40: La jeune Academie du cinéma français," *Cinéma 58*, 24 (February 1958): 5.
11. Ibid.: 21.
12. One theater owner in Dayton, Ohio was even arrested on obscenity charges for screening Malle's movie; the Ohio Supreme Court later overturned his conviction to serve time on a prison farm and pay a fine.
13. François Truffaut, "A Certain Tendency of the French Cinema," in Joanne Hollows, Peter Hutchings, and Mark Joncovich, eds., *The Film Studies Reader* (London: Arnold, 2000), pp. 58–62.

Chapter 2 A Critical Concept

1. François Truffaut, "Interview," *Arts* 720 (March 20, 1959).
2. "Jean-Luc Godard," *Cahiers du Cinéma* 138 (December 1962): 21.
3. Claude Chabrol, *Et pourtant je tourne* (Paris: Robert Laffont, 1976), p. 135.
4. Alexandre Astruc, "The birth of a new avant-garde: la caméra-stylo," in Peter Graham, ed., *The New Wave* (Garden City, NJ: Doubleday, 1968), p. 17.

5. Ibid., p. 20.

6. Jean-Luc Godard, *Godard on Godard*, trans. Tom Milne (New York: Viking, 1972), p. 96.

7. François Truffaut, "A Certain Tendency of the French Cinema," in Bill Nichols, ed., *Movies and Methods* (Berkeley: University of California Press, 1976), p. 225.

8. Ibid.

9. Ibid., p. 226.

10. Ibid., pp. 228–9.

11. Ibid., p. 229.

12. Raymond Radiguet, *Devil in the Flesh*, trans. Kay Boyle (New York: Signet, 1955), p. 24.

13. Truffaut, "A Certain Tendency," p. 229.

14. Ibid., p. 233.

15. Alexandre Astruc, *Le Montreur d'ombres, mémoires* (Paris: Bartillat, 1996), p. 136.

16. Ibid.

17. Godard, *Godard on Godard*, p. 96.

18. François Truffaut, "Ali Baba et la 'Politique des auteurs'," *Cahiers du Cinéma* 44 (February 1955): 45–7.

19. André Bazin, "Comment peut-on être Hitchcocko-Hawksien?" *Cahiers du Cinéma* 44 (February 1955): 18.

20. Ibid.

21. Jean-Luc Godard, et al., "Hiroshima, notre amour," *Cahiers du Cinéma* 97 (July 1959): 11; reprinted in Jim Hillier, ed., *Cahiers du Cinéma: The 1950s* (Cambridge: Harvard University Press, 1985), p. 62.

22. Jacques Rivette, "De l'abjection (Kapo)," *Cahiers du Cinéma* 120 (June 1961): 54.

23. Francis Courtade, *Les Malédictions du cinéma français* (Paris: Alain Moreau, 1978) and Freddy Buache, *Le Cinéma français des années soixante* (Paris: Hatier, 1987).

Chapter 3 A Mode of Production and Distribution

1. For more on budgets of 1950s films, see the valuable article by H. C. Hagenthaler, "Spécial cinéma français," *Esprit* (June 1960). All costs are cited

in old francs, which typically are transferred at an exchange rate of $2,000 per one million *ancien francs*.

2. "Jean-Pierre Melville, 'inventeur' de la nouvelle vague," *Cinéma 60*, 46 (May 1960): 23–6.

3. Agnès Varda's radio interview, cited in *Varda par Agnès* (Paris: Cahiers du Cinéma, 1994), p. 227.

4. Roger Leenhardt, in André Bazin et al., "Six personnages en quête d'auteurs," *Cahiers du Cinéma* 71 (May 1957): 24.

5. Jacques Rivette, in *ibid*. Note: this section is omitted from the translated version of "Six Characters in Search of Auteurs" printed in Jim Hillier, ed., *Cahiers du Cinéma: The 1950s* (Cambridge: Harvard University Press, 1985), pp. 31–46.

6. Hillier, *Cahiers du Cinema*, p. 34.

7. Ibid., p. 40.

8. Claude Chabrol, *Et Pourtant je tourne* (Paris: Laffont, 1976), p. 136.

9. Edgar Morin, "*Chronique d'un été*," in *France-Observateur* "Domaine Cinéma," 1 (Winter, 1961–2).

10. Luc Moullet, "Trois points d'économie," *Cahiers du Cinéma* 138 (December 1962): 88.

Chapter 4 A Technical Practice, an Aesthetic

1. Alexandre Astruc, "The birth of a new avant-garde: la caméra stylo," in Peter Graham, ed., *The New Wave* (Garden City, NJ: Doubleday, 1968), p. 22.

2. For more on Truffaut and his work with scriptwriters, see Carole Le Berre, *François Truffaut* (Paris: Cahiers du Cinéma, 1993).

3. See Antoine de Baecque, "La Politique des copains," in *Pour un cinéma comparé* (Paris: La Cinémathèque française), pp. 208–9.

4. Jean Gruault, *Ce que dit l'autre* (Paris: Juillard, 1992).

5. Jonathan Rosenbaum, ed., *Rivette: Texts and Interviews* (London: British Film Institute, 1977), p. 43.

6. Claude Chabrol, *Et pourtant je tourne* (Paris: Laffont, 1976), pp. 140–1.

7. Robert Benayoun, "The king is naked," in Peter Graham, ed., *The New Wave* (Garden City, NJ: Doubleday, 1968), p. 163.

8. Chabrol, *Et pourtant je tourne*, p. 140.

9. Ibid.; this story was initially told in "An interview," *Arts* (February 19, 1958).

10. Chabrol, *Et pourtant je tourne*, pp. 139–140.

11. Antoine de Baecque and Serge Toubiana, *Truffaut*, trans. Catherine Temerson (New York: Alfred A. Knopf, 1999), p. 128.

12. Vincent Rogard, "Raoul Coutard," in Jean Luc Douin, ed., *La Nouvelle Vague 25 ans après* (Paris: CERF, 1983), p. 119.

13. Raoul Coutard gave a detailed interview on the process that was published in *Nouvel Observateur* (September 22, 1965).

14. Jean-Luc Godard, "Feu sur *Les Carabiniers*," *Cahiers du Cinéma* 146 (August 1963): 2–3.

15. Maxime Scheinfeigel, "Eclats de voix," *Admiranda* 10 (1995).

16. For more on Rozier's production methods, see Nicole Zand, "Le dossier Philippine," *Cahiers du cinéma* 148 (October 1963): 32–9.

Chapter 5 New Themes and New Bodies

1. "Marivaudage" is a French term, derived from the literary style of Pierre de Marivaux, (1688–1763), whose plays often featured flirtatious banter and dialogue set in a refined environment; Saganism refers to the fictional world of Françoise Sagan's contemporary fiction involving the sexual antics of the modern era.

2. Alexandre Astruc and Philippe D'Hugues, *Le Montreur d'ombres, mémoires* (Paris: Bartillat, 1996), p. 280.

3. Jacques Siclier, *Nouvelle vague?* (Paris: Cerf, 1961), p. 98.

4. For a wonderful review, see Barthélemy Amengual, "Le réalisme des *Amants* ou les papiers collés du Tendre," reprinted in *Du réalisme au cinéma* (Paris: Nathan, 1997). See also Richard Neupert, *The French New Wave* (Madison: University of Wisconsin Press, 2002).

5. Antoine de Baecque and Serge Toubiana, *Truffaut*, trans. Catherine Temerson (New York: Knopf, 1999), pp. 172–3.

6. Freddy Buache, *Nouvelle Vague* (Paris: Terrain Vague, 1962), p. 61.

7. For more on Truffaut's world and cinéphilia, see Anne Gillain, *François Truffaut: Le Secret perdu* (Paris: Hatier, 1991).

8. Luis Buñuel, *Mon dernier soupir* (Paris: Robert Laffont, 1994), p. 299.

9. Raymond Borde, *Nouvelle Vague* (Paris: Premier Plan, 1962), pp. 20–1.

10. Robert Benayoun "Dictionnaire partiel et partial d'un nouveau Cinéma Français," *Positif* 46 (June 1962): 27.

11. Jean-Louis Bory, "*Adieu Philippine*," *Arts* (2 October 1963).

Chapter 6 The New Wave's International Influence and Legacy Today

1. See Jean-Louis Leutrat, *Le Cinéma en perspective: une histoire* (Paris: Nathan, 1992), pp. 47–53.
2. Barthélemy Amengual, "Les Nouvelles vagues," in Claude Beylie and Philippe Carcassonne, eds., *Le Cinéma* (Paris: Bordas, 1983), p. 64.
3. Jacques Rivette, "Lettre sur Rossellini," *Cahiers du Cinéma* 46 (April 1955): 14–15.
4. Raymond Borde, "Préface," to Francis Courtade, *Les Malédictions du cinéma français* (Paris: Alain Moreau, 1978).

Appendix

1. For a fuller version, see Anne Simonin and Hélène Clastres, eds., *Les Idées en France (1945–1988)* (Paris: Gallimard, 1989).

Bibliography

Sources from the New Wave Era (1957–63)

The entire output of *Cahiers du Cinéma* as well as of *Cinéma* and *Positif* during this period are certainly important; however, the following issues are particularly pertinent:

Cahiers du Cinéma

- #71 (May 1957): "Situation du cinéma français," "Six personnages en quête d'auteurs," and a interview with Jacques Flaud, director of the CNC at the time;
- #138 (December 1962): This "Nouvelle Vague" special issue contains interviews with Claude Chabrol, Jean-Luc Godard, and François Truffaut, as well as a "dictionary" of 162 French filmmakers;
- #161–2 (January 1965): special issue on the crisis of French cinema.

Cinéma

- *Cinéma 58* #24 (February 1958): special inquiry into the young generation of French cinema;
- *Cinéma 64* #88 (July–August 1964): special issue on "Ten years of French Cinema."

Positif

- #46 (June 1962): Examination of recent trends: "Feux sur le cinéma français."

Other French journals from the era are also valuable, including the weeklies dedicated to culture, such as *France-Observateur* and *Express*, while *Arts-spectacles* and *Lettres françaises* also contain very helpful references. See also *Esprit*'s 1960 special issue on French cinema, including "Le système de production," by H. C. Hagenthaler, and "Comment d'autres fabriquent des brosses à dents," with an interview with René Thévenet.

Three Important Publications that Came out during the Era

Labarthe, André S., *Essai sur le jeune cinéma français* (Paris: Le Terrain Vague, 1960).
   The first stimulating "reflections on a wave" are offered by Labarthe, who was a colleague from *Cahiers* and a future director of television and documentaries.
Siclier, Jacques, *Nouvelle vague?* (Paris: Cerf, 1961).
   This invaluable, 136-page packet has two very rich chapters, including the section on economics, though the third section on the world of the New Wave is more debatable.
Borde, Raymond, Freddy Buache, and Jean Curtelin, *Nouvelle Vague* (Lyon: Serdoc, 1962).
   A violent pamphlet, in three parts, attacking the New Wave and its *Cahiers du Cinéma* connections, written by critics allied with *Positif*.

Central Histories of the New Wave and French Cinema of the Period

Baecque, Antoine de, *La Nouvelle Vague: portrait d'une jeunesse* (Paris: Flammarion, 1998).
Buache, Freddy, *Le Cinéma français des années soixante* (Paris: Cinq Continents / Hatier, 1987).
   Emphasizes the social-political context.
Clouzot, Claire, *Le Cinéma français depuis la nouvelle vague* (Paris: Nathan, 1972).
   A very didactic synthesis.
Courtade, Francis, *Les Malédictions du cinéma français* (Paris: Alain Moreau, 1978).
   For a study supposedly presenting a social history, it is very antagonistic to *Cahiers du Cinéma*.

Douin, Jean-Luc, ed., *La Nouvelle Vague 25 ans après* (Paris: Cerf, 1983).

The first part contains many interesting historical essays, followed by many first-person, eye-witness accounts that must be read more critically.

Frodon, Jean-Michel, *L'Age moderne du cinéma français, de la Nouvelle Vague à nos jours* (Paris: Flammarion, 1995).

A very long, informative account of the developments surrounding the New Wave, young French cinema, and modern cinema.

Jeancolas, Jean-Pierre, *Le Cinéma français, la Ve Républic, 1958–1978* (Paris: Stock, 1979).

A solid, 480-page, institutional history.

——*Histoire du cinéma français* (Paris: Nathan (128 Series), 1995).

Prédal, René, *Cinquante ans de cinéma français* (Paris: Nathan, 1996).

A huge, 1,006-page overview of 50 years of French cinema which includes a complete list of all French films produced between 1945 and 1995.

Sadoul, Georges, *Le Cinéma français, 1890–1962* (Paris: Flammarion, 1962).

A great deal of statistical information in a 292-page history.

Turigliano, Roberto, ed., *Nouvelle Vague* (Turin: Festival internazionale Cinema Giovani, 1985).

The only real encyclopedia of the New Wave, published 25 years after the fact. Originally in Italian, it has been translated into several languages.

Critical Histories

Andrew, Dudley, *André Bazin* (New York: Oxford University Press, 1978).

A very valuable biography.

Baecque, Antoine de, *Cahiers du Cinéma, histoire d'une revue*, vols I and II (Paris: Cahiers du Cinéma, 1991, 1995).

Very detailed histories of *Cahiers du Cinéma*, seen from within.

Economic Histories and Histories of Producers

Beauregard, Chantal de, *Georges de Beauregard* (Nimes: C. Lacour, 1991).

A very personal biography written by the producer's daughter.

Bonnell, René, *Le Cinéma exploité* (Paris: Seuil, 1978).

The best reference book for an economic history of the period.

Braunberger, Pierre and Jacques Gerber, *Cinémamémoire* (Paris: Centre Georges Pompidou/CNC, 1987).
  A personal recollection with many documents included.
Crisp, Colin, *The Classic French Cinema: 1930–1960* (Bloomington: Indiana University Press, 1993).
Dauman, Anatole and Jacques Gerber, *Souvenir écran* (Paris: Centre Georges Pompidou, 1989).

Scriptwriters

Gruault, Jean, *Ce que dit l'autre* (Paris: Julliard, 1992).
  A very rich autobiographical account by an important collaborator of Truffaut, Rossellini, Godard, Rivette, and Resnais.

Directors

Writings, interviews, critical anthologies, memoires, collected letters

Astruc, Alexandre, *Du stylo à la caméra* (Paris: Archipel, 1992).
  A collection of Astruc's major essays.
Astruc, Alexandre and Philippe D'Hugues, *Le Montreur d'ombres, mémoires* (Paris: Bartillat, 1996).
  While the anecdotes would all have to be verified, this book proves Astruc still has a great style.
Chabrol, Claude, *Et pourtant je tourne* (Paris: Laffont, 1976).
  Chabrol's memoirs, recollected along with the help of René Marchand, are retold in a fairly off-hand and chatty format.
Godard, Jean-Luc, *Godard on Godard*, trans. Tom Milne (New York: Viking, 1972).
  An incredibly valuable anthology which includes all Godard's critical essays and some interviews.
——*Introduction à une véritable histoire du cinéma* (Paris: Albatros, 1980).
Melville, Jean-Pierre and Rui Nogueira, *Le Cinéma selon Melville* (Paris: Seghers, 1974).
  A book based on interviews.

Rohmer, Eric, *Le Gout de la beauté* (Paris: Cahiers du Cinéma, 1984).
An anthology of many of Rohmer's critical articles.
Gillain, Anne, *Le Cinéma selon François Truffaut* (Paris: Flammarion, 1988).
An anthology of Truffaut's principal interviews, collected and edited by Anne Gillain.
Truffaut, François, *Correspondence 1945–1984*, ed., Gilles Jacob and Claude de Givray, trans.
Gilbert Adair (New York: Noonday Press, 1990).
—— *The Films of My Life*, trans. Leonard Mayhew (New York: Simon and Schuster, 1978).
Chapter 5, on his particiption in the New Wave, is particularly pertinent.
Varda, Agnès, *Varda par Agnès* (Paris: Cahiers du Cinéma, 1994).

Critical studies of auteurs

Bellour, Raymond, *Alexandre Astruc* (Paris: Seghers, 1963).
Boiron, Pierre, *Pierre Kast* (Paris: Lherminier, 1985).

Studies of Claude Chabrol

Braucourt, Claude, *Claude Chabrol* (Paris: Seghers, 1971).
Blanchet, Christian, *Claude Chabrol* (Paris: Rivages, 1989).
Magny, Joel, *Claude Chabrol* (Paris: Cahiers du Cinéma, 1987).

Studies of Jean-Luc Godard

Bellour, Raymond and Marie-Léa Bandy. *Jean-Luc Godard, Son + Image, 1974–1991* (New York: Museum of Modern Art, 1992).
This collection is devoted entirely to Godard's video period and films from *Everyman for Himself* up to 1991.
Cerisuelo, Marc, *Jean-Luc Godard* (Paris: Lherminier, 1989).
—— ed., "Jean-Luc Godard, au-delà des images," *Etudes cinématographiques* 194/202 (1993).
Collet, Jean, *Jean-Luc Godard* (Paris: Seghers, 1963).
Subsequently re-issued in several editions, Collet's book provided the first intelligent monograph of Godard's work, written just after *Contempt* in 1963.
Douin, Jean-Luc, *Jean-Luc Godard* (Paris: Rivages, 1989).

Dubois, Philippe, ed., "Jean-Luc Godard, les films," *Revue Belge du cinéma* 16 (Summer, 1986).

——ed., "Jean-Luc Godard, le cinéma," *Revue Belge du cinéma* 22/23 (1989). A very expanded version of the earlier issue.

Estève, Michel, ed., "Jean-Luc Godard, au-delà du récit," *Etudes Cinématographiques* 57–61 (1967).

Prédal, René, ed., *CinémAction* 52 (July 1989).

Toffetti, Sergio, ed., *Jean-Luc Godard* (Turin: Cultural Center and National Museum of Cinema, 1990).

Studies of Eric Rohmer

Bonitzer, Pascal, *Eric Rohmer* (Paris: Cahiers du Cinéma, 1991).

Estève, Michel, ed., "Eric Rohmer 1 et 2," *Etudes cinématographiques* 146/148 (1985) and 149/152 (1986).

Magny, Joel, *Eric Rohmer* (Paris: Rivages, 1986).

Studies of Jacques Rivette

Frappat, Hélène, *Jacques Rivette, secret compris* (Paris: Cahiers du Cinéma, 2001).

Toffetti, Sergio, ed., *Jacques Rivette, la règle du jeu* (Turin: Cultural Center and National Museum of Cinema, 1992).

Studies of Jean Rouch

Prédal, René, ed., "Jean Rouch, le ciné-plaisir," *CinémAction* 81 (1996).

——"Jean Rouch, un griot gaulois," *CinémAction* 17 (February 1981).

Studies of François Truffaut

Cahoreau, Gilles, *François Truffaut, 1932–1984* (Paris: Julliard, 1989).

Baecque, Antoine de and Serge Toubiana, *François Truffaut* (Paris: Gallimard, 1996).

At 666 pages, this is a quasi-posthumous autobiography, since it is based on material gathered by the director himself before his death.

Gillain, Anne, *François Truffaut* (Paris: Hatier, 1991).
  A brilliant psycho-biographical analysis of the director's oeuvre.
Le Berre, Carole, *François Truffaut* (Paris: Cahiers du Cinéma, 1993).
  Valuable for its study of the genesis of the films.

Dossiers and Studies of Individual Films

One additional source to consult is *L'Avant-Scène*, which has devoted more than 100 issues to the decoupages and scripts of films by New Wave directors. Two "ciné-romans" that help prove the renown of these films when they were released, are Jehanne, Jean-Charles, *Les Cousins*, "*shock novel*," (Paris: Seghers, 1959), based on Claude Chabrol's film and Paul Gégauff's dialogues; and Francolin, Claude, *A Bout de souffle*, "*shock novel*," (Paris: Seghers, 1960), based on the work of Jean-Luc Godard, François Truffaut, and Claude Chabrol.
Other monographs devoted to individual films include:
Amengual, Barthélemy, *Bande à part de Jean-Luc Godard* (Crisnée, Belgium: Yellow Now, 1993).
Cieutat, Michel, *Pierrot le fou de Jean-Luc Godard* (Paris: Limonest, 1993).
Gillain, Anne, *Les Quatre Cents Coups de François Truffaut* (Paris: Nathan, 1991).
Leutrat, Jean-Louis, *Hiroshima mon amour d'Alain Resnais* (Paris: Nathan, 1994).
Rouch, Jean and Edgar Morin, *Chronique d'un été* (Paris: InterSpectacles, 1962).
Vaugeois, Gérard, ed., *A Bout de souffle* (Paris: Balland, 1974).

English-Language Sources

Andrew, Dudley, ed., *Breathless* (New Brunswick, NJ: Rutgers University Press, 1995).
Armes, Roy, *French Cinema* (London: Secker and Warburg, 1985).
——*French Cinema Since 1946* (New Jersey: A. S. Barnes, 1970).
Austin, Guy, *Claude Chabrol* (Manchester: Manchester University Press, 1999).
Bazin, André, *French Cinema of the Occupation and Resistance,* trans. Stanley Hochman (New York: Frederick Ungar, 1981).
Brown, Royal S., *Focus on Godard* (Englewood Cliffs: Prentice-Hall, 1972).
Cameron, Ian, ed., *The Films of Jean-Luc Godard* (New York: Praeger, 1970).
Crisp, Colin, *The Classic French Cinema, 1930–1960* (Bloomington: Indiana University Press, 1993).

——*Eric Rohmer: Realist and Moralist* (Bloomington: Indiana University Press, 1988).

de Baecque, Antoine and Serge Toubiana, *Truffaut*, trans. Catherine Temerson (New York: Alfred A. Knopf, 1999). (Original version, *Francois Truffaut* (Paris: Gallimard, 1996).)

Dixon, Wheeler Winston, *The Early Film Criticism of François Truffaut* (Bloomington: Indiana University Press, 1993).

—— *The Films of Jean-Luc Godard* (Albany: State University of New York Press, 1997).

Douchet, Jean, *French New Wave*, trans. Robert Bonnono (New York: Distributed Art Publishers, 1999).

Godard, Jean-Luc, *Godard on Godard*, trans. Tom Milne (New York: Viking, 1972).

Graham, Peter, ed., *The New Wave* (Garden City, NY: Doubleday, 1968).

Hayward, Susan, *French National Cinema* (London: Routledge, 1993).

Hillier, Jim, ed., *Cahiers du Cinéma: The 1960s* (Cambridge, MA: Harvard University Press, 1992).

Hogue, Peter, "Melville: The Elective Affinities," *Film Comment* (November–December, 1996): 17–22.

Holmes, Diana and Robert Ingram, *François Truffaut* (New York: Manchester University Press, 1998).

Insdorf, Annette, *François Truffaut* (New York: Cambridge University Press, 1994).

Kline, T. Jefferson, *Screening the Text: Intertextuality in New Wave French Cinema* (Baltimore: Johns Hopkins University Press, 1992).

Larkin, Maurice, *France Since the Popular Front* (Oxford: Clarendon Press, 1988).

Monaco, James, *The New Wave* (New York: Oxford University Press, 1976).

Neupert, Richard, "Dead Champagne: *Variety*'s New Wave," *Film History* 10, 2 (1998): 219–30.

——*A History of the French New Wave* (Madison: University of Wisconsin Press, 2002).

Nicholls, David, *François Truffaut* (London: B. T. Batsford, 1993).

Raboudin, Dominique, ed., *Truffaut by Truffaut*, Trans. Robert Erich Wolf (New York: Harry N. Abrams, 1987).

Rohmer, Eric, *The Taste of Beauty*, trans. Carol Volk (Cambridge: Cambridge University Press, 1989).

Roud, Richard, *Godard* (Bloomington: Indiana University Press, 1970).

Sterritt, David, *The Films of Jean-Luc Godard: Seeing the Invisible* (Cambridge: Cambridge University Press, 1999).

Truffaut, François, *The Films of My Life* (New York: Simon and Schuster, 1975).

Vincendeau, Ginette, *The Companion to French Cinema* (London: Cassell and British Film Institute, 1996).

—— *Stars and Stardom in French Cinema* (New York: Continuum International Publishing, 2000).

Williams, Alan, *Republic of Images: A History of French Filmmaking* (Cambridge, MA: Harvard University Press, 1992).

Index